Portrayal of Pakistan by U.S. Leading News Magazines

ZAFAR ALI

DEDICATION

"This work is dedicated to my beloved parents, who passed on a love of reading and respect for education"

CONTENTS

ACKNOWLEDGMENTS

Special thanks to the distinguished faculty members of Center for Media Studies. I would like to state my cordial admiration and thanks to all the friends and classmates who helped me through various step in this research. I express gratitude to pleasant support and guidance of my supervisor Prof. Dr. Saqib Riaz, Department of Mass Communication, Allama Iqbal Open University, Islamabad.

I also wish to sincerely admit the precious advice and motivation by Prof. Dr. Zafar Iqbal, Center for Media and communication, International Islamic University Islamabad. My special gratitude is due to my friends who inspirations encourage me in research. And special thanks to my parents for their prayers and good-natured patience with the process and for their pride in this accomplishment.

Finally, I would like to thank everybody who was important to the successful realization of thesis, as well as expressing my apology that I could not mention personally one by one.

1 INTRODUCTION

Communication is an essential part of human communication. Print media is a tool of communication. We know that the media is a mirror of the society. Its primary function is to provide the news and views to audience. Through this way media influence the society. Media plays a significant role in the socialization of the individuals. Historically written words had their importance in the world as they can be presented for references more reliably. All the media organizations have their own perception or the point of view in selecting or rejecting any news story or article. Selection and editing of any news items according to personal observation is called "Gate keeping". Gatekeeper may be the reporter, editor, anchor or producers in any media organization. They frame any news story or issue in the media in particular point of view. Behind framing there is another driving force of agenda setter which set the media agenda, that what should be present to the audience.

Media organizations have the powerful influence in making and mould the public opinion. Print media set his agenda on the opinion pages. They frame the news issues according to their agenda. Impact of modern technologies shrunk the world as "Global Village". In this way people come to know that what media expose to them on media. They determine their opinion on the basis of their exposure. In the global war against terrorism, media has become an important battlefield. Pakistan is an Islamic democratic country who is facing terrorism from many years.

The entire world comes to be familiar with what the media expose to them. In the West there are many misconceptions about the Pakistan. Were these misconceptions portrayed by the western media? These were the questions which arise in researcher mind. In this study researcher tries to meet these questions.

Top two leading news magazines of US are selected for the rationale of this research. These magazines have not only vast readership in US but also in the whole world. Editorial and opinion pages have strong influence in making the opinion of readers. Content analysis of both magazines of six month is studied for this research. The data is collected from primary sources. The primary objective of this study is to find the image of Pakistan in the US leading news magazines. Content of both magazines were analyzed for this study. Berelson (1952) quoted definition, "Content analysis is a research technique for the objective, systematic, and quantitative description of the manifest content of communication"

The dawn of the freedom of Pakistan was the implementation of the idea of Pakistan. The idea for the birth of Pakistan was "Two Nation Theory." That was the idea that the Muslims minority of the subcontinent should have got their own state on the basis of religion. Otherwise the Hindu majority of the subcontinent will rule on the Muslims. Islamic Republic of Pakistan was emerged on map of the world in Auguast14, 1947 (International Media Support, 2009).

Geographically Pakistan is situated in the South Asia. Its total area is 796096 sq km. The world's second highest mountains peek K-2 is situated in the north of the country. In the middle rich agriculture fields watered by five rivers and in the south vast desert are placed (Yasin 2010). Pak land heritage four season that are, summer, winter, autumn and spring. Islamabad is the capital city of Pakistan.

Total estimated population of Pakistan on 1st January, 2009 was, 163.76 million where male were 84.98 and female 78.78 million (Statpak, 2010). Ethnic groups in Pakistan: Punjabi, Sindhi, Pashtun, Baloch, Muhajir (i.e., Urdu-speaking immigrants from India and their descendants), Saraiki, and Hazara. Languages mostly spoken in the Pakistan are "Urdu (national and official), English, Punjabi, Sindhi, Pashto, Baloch, Hindko, Brahui, Saraiki (Punjabi variant)" (CIA, 2009).

1.1 Education, Literacy

Pakistan Social and Living Standards Measurement (PSLM) survey 2008-9 shown literacy rate as, 57% whereas male 69% and female were 45%. PSLM data shows that literacy rate in urban areas (75%) is higher than he the rural areas (48%). Provincially Punjab stood 59%, Sindh 59%, Khyber Pakhtunkhwa 50% and Baluchistan at 45% (Economic Survey 2009-10).

1.2 Health

Infant mortality rate in 2008 was 66.95/1,000. Life expectancy in men was 63.07 years and in Women 65.24 yrs (CIA, 2009). According to government report in 2008 number of Hospitals 948, Dispensaries 4794,

M.C.H. Centers 908, Rural Health Centers 561 and Basic Health Units were 5310. In there 133956 doctor and 91221 paramedical staff were serving (Pakistan, Introduction 2006).

1.3 Pakistan Media

Pakistan media is divided into two major categories; print media and electronic media.

1.3.1 The Print Media

Major Online Urdu Newspaper
Urdu Point, Akhbar-e-Jehan, Al-Akhbar, Apnajpj, BBC News, Chitral News, Daily Alfazl, Daily ASAS, Daily Ausaf, Daily Awami Awaz, Daily Express, Daily Gujranwala Times , Daily Intekhab, Daily Imroz, Daily islam, Daily Jang, Daily Millat Gujarati & Urdu , The Daily Jasarat, Daily Maizbaan, Daily Jinnah, Daily Khabrain, Daily Mashriq, Daily Pakistan, Daily Shana Bashana, Jasarat, Daily Ummat, Kasheer, Millat Online, Minhaj-ul-Quran, Tasweer-E-Wattan, Nawa-e-Islam, Nawai-i-WaqtAl Qamar (PID, 2010).

Major Online English Newspaper
The Asia Inside, Associated Press of Pakistan Attock News, Balochistan Post, Business Recorder, Daily Balochistan Express, Daily Financial Post, Daily Hot News, Daily Independent, Daily Ibrat, [In Sindhi]Daily Kawish [In Sindhi], The Daily Leader International, Daily Mail, Daily Pakistan News, Daily Times, Dawn, The Friday Times, The Frontier Post, Herald, Hi Pakistan, International News Network, Isponline, Jhelum News, Jhelum Times, Kashmir Media Service, Kashmir Observer, Khyber Mail, Lovely Pakistan, The Nation, The News International, News Network International, Pakistan Link, Pakistan Observer, PakTribune, Sindh Today, South Asia Tribune, The Statesman, Times, Times of Pakistan, Weekly Asia, Weekly Independent (pakreview, 2010).

Major English Language Magazines
Chef Special International, Jahangir World Times, Bulletin, V SHINE International, Relic, Ink Magazine, Business Magazine, Brand New, Seasons & Style, Humsay, Alqadeer, Herald, Internet, More Magazine, Moorad Shipping News, Newsline, Spider, Game Mode, The Cricketer, Joules, TecknowMag, Campus Magazine, Pakistan Textile Journal, Property Standard, Hospital Magazine, Youth Circle, She Magazine, Libas, Brides

and You, Me and my Wedding, Smash, IBEX, Construction Trends, Living Express, Pak Euro World, Women Magazine (Wikepedia).

Major Urdu language Magazines

Chef Special Pakistan's Leading Cooking Magazine, Mahnama Kitchen , Mystery Magazine, Friday Special, Monthly Adventure, Notebook, Khabeer, Al-Turka, Zanjeer, Bang-e-Jars, Durdarshan, Awami Jamhori Forum, Aanchal, Adventure, Akhbar e Jahan, Falak Rang, Asia, Audio Video Satellite, Computing, Durdarshan, Dharb-i-Mumin, Diva, Family,Global Science, Hikayat, Hina, Kiran, Kitchen, Lazzat, Motherhood, Nida e Millat, Nigar, Pakistan Post, Sathi, Shama, Shoa,Shuaa,Super Star Dust, Suspense Digest, Urdu Digest, Visage, Piyam-e-Dar-Us-Salam, Jab-e-Adab, Wasta International, Falak Rang, Masoom, Nisab, Noor,Phool, Saathi, Jasoosi, Rafta Rafta, Taleem-o-Tarbiat" (wikepedia).

1.3.2   Electronic Media

TV Channels

Television is a widely used media in the world for quick and live coverage of many issues and news. In October 1963, government of Pakistan signed an agreement with the NEC (Nippon Electronic Company) to installation of PTV setup. First TV station started its broadcasting in Pakistan on November26, 1964 at the city of Lahore. Later on in 1967 Karachi and Islamabad/Rawalpindi and in 1972 Peshawar and Quetta stations started their transmissions. PTV network contain following g channels.

PTV Home, PTV News, PTV National, PTV Global, PTV Prime, PTV Bolan, AJK TV, ATV, AVT Khyber. While in Pakistan first time educational TV is working under the Virtual University satellite television. It contains four channels like VU 1, VU 2, VU 3 and VU 4 in MCPC mode.

Pervaze Mushraf' government has decided to lift the ban on private media ownership in Pakistan in 2000. Many stations have started their transmission and got extreme popularity in the masses. Following are the private TV channels in Pakistan which provide news and views, information and entertainment to the audience.

Aag , Aaj TV, Aljazeera Urdu, Apna Channel, ARY Bangla, ARY Digital, ARY One World, , Business Plus, Channel G, CNBC Pakistan, Dawn News, DM Digital Network, Duniya TV, Express Media Network, Eye Television Network, Fashion TV Pakistan, Filmazia, Geo TV Network, Geo Super, Haq TV, HBO Pakistan, Hum TV, Indus TV Network, Indus Vision, Indus Music, Indus News, Labbaik TV, Mashriq TV, Music One, MTV Pakistan, Nawawaqt Group of Publications, nVibe, Play, QTV, Rohi TV, Roshni TV, Royal TV, Rung TV, Sun Entertainment, Sindh TV, The Musik, TV 2 Day, TV One, Ujala TV (Pakrewiew, 2010).

Radio AM, FM

This is the age of information and communication and radio is the most important medium of communication. It plays a vital role in development where literacy rate is low and in remote areas of the country. Radio is a very successful tool of communication in remote areas of the country. As the literacy rate is low so radio is very important way of communication. The other ways of communication are sometime not effective. The Pakistan Broadcasting Corporation has played a vital role in disseminating awareness and broadcasting the policies of government. It promoted the national ideology and patriotism in the masses. It covers more than 80 percent of the population (countrystudies, 2010).

The origin of broadcasting in subcontinent goes back to 1927 when Bombay station of the Indian Broadcasting Service was inaugurated. In 1928 a small station was installed under YMCA (Ahmad, 2009) while in 1935 Peshawar Broadcasting station was launched. At the time of independence there were three radio stations in Pakistan Peshawar, Lahore and Dhaka (capital of Bangladesh). In Pakistan broadcasting was initiated by Pakistan Broadcasting Service. Later it has become Radio Pakistan and subsequently Pakistan Broadcasting Corporation (PBC) on 20th Dec.1972.

Technically there are two types of Radio broadcasting one is AM (amplified modulation) and FM (frequency modulation). AM radio stations, are most common and have a greater broadcasting range. This is the oldest medium in radio broadcasting. FM radio stations are modern and upcoming technology providing superior tonal quality, especially in regard to music and free from static.). There are 26 AM radio station and more than 60 FM radio stations network in Pakistan.

AM channels in the cities of Pakistan: Islamabad, Rawalpindi, Lahore, Multan, Faisalabad, Bahawalpur, Peshawar, Dera Ismail Khan, Abbottabad, Chitrial, Sakardu, Quetta, Sibi, Khuzdar, Turbat, Karachi, Hyderabad, Khairpur.

FM Radio Channels Network

Network of FM 101: Islamabad, Rawalpindi, Lahore, Faisalabad, Sialkot, Sargodha, Mianwali, Peshawar, Hyderabad, Karachi, Bannu, Kohat, Quetta and Gwadar.

Network of FM 100: Islamabad, Rawalpindi, Lahore and Karachi.

Network of MAST FM 103: Lahore, Faisalabad, Karachi and Multan.

Network of Radio Buraq: FM104, Sialkot, Peshawar, Mardan and Punjab University FM104, Lahore.

AWAZ Radio FM Network: FM104 at Bhalwal-Sargodha, Rajanpur, FM

5

105 at Gujrat, Bahawalpur, Jhang and Sadiqabad, FM106 at Gujranwala and Khanpur.

City FM 99 Network: Islamabad, Rawalpindi, Lahore, Faisalabad, Karachi.

1.4   Economy of Pakistan

In the face of rigorous challenges, the economy has shown flexibility in the passing year. Growth in Gross Domestic Product (GDP) for 2009-10, on an inflation adjusted basis, has been recorded at a provisional 4.1%. This compares with GDP growth of 1.2% in the previous year.

Pakistan has five neighbour countries, Afghanistan bordered by 2430 km in south, in the east India having bordered of 2912 km, Iran is situated in the west of Pakistan bordered by 909 km and in the far northeast People Republic of China is situated, While Tajikistan also lies close to Pakistan near Wakhan corridor (CIA, 2009).

Pakistan is situated in the heart of ancient Indus Valley Civilization. Indus Valley subjected to frequent invader as well as Alexander, the Great. But the region flourished in the kingdom of Mughal in 17th centuries. British regime has taken over the subcontinent from the 18th century. That has ended with the partition of subcontinent in 1947 (Statpak, 2006). Islam was the driving force behind the establishment of Pakistan. Therefore, Islam is the state religion of Pakistan. About 95% of the Pakistanis are Muslim (Sunni 75%, Shia 20%), other are includes Christian and Hindu 5% (CIA, 2009).

Constitutional development of Pakistan has promulgated three constitutions, in 1956, 1962 and 1973 respectively since the independence of the country. In the period of the last 63 years, 'three Martial Laws and one military Quasi have been imposed by the military ruler for more than 30 years' (Ali, 2008).

Secretary General of the United Nations, Ban Ki Moon once said that,"the two most dangerous countries on this planet are Pakistan and Afghanistan" (Jafri, 2009). Pakistan faced cruelty of terrorist where hundred people are assassinated in the suicide attacks. Pakistan armed forces are hit by terrorist in all parts of the countries. These terrorist hit the educational institutions, shopping centers and prayer houses of people having diverse ideology and faiths in Pakistan.

1.5   The Impact of 9/11 on Pakistan

The dreadful event of 9/11 once again influences on the image of Pakistan in the world. Before the incident of 9/11 Pakistan had recognized the Talban government in Afghanistan. But as the incident of 9/11

6

occurred US president Gorge W. Bush declared the war against terrorism. Al-Qaida was accused for the destructive attacks of 9/11. As Afghanistan Talban government had the close link with Al-Qaeda and host of Osama Bin Laden a leader of Al-Qaeda. Osama was the main actor in Afghan jihad war against Russian's invasion.

It is historically approved that in cold war US supported the jihadi organization in Afghanistan. In Pakistan US government support the military ruler Gen. Zia-ul-haq in establishing and promoting jihadi organization on the land of Pakistan. US government has supported these organizations through funds and arms against Russia. Its core rationale was to stop the Russian invasion in the region. US had emboldened the Muslin fanaticism about jihad. "Islamism" implanted in the functioning of the country under military rule. The tent of "Islamic fundamentalism" sponsored by US intelligence were adopted by military dictatorship of General Zia, with a view to undermining the structure of the civilian government and the rule of law (Global Research, 2010).but after Russia's quit from Afghanistan, US once left these trained jihadi alone and stopped to aid them.

After the tragedy of 9/11 US labels that Al-Qaeda was responsible of these terrible attacks. US president G.W. Bush declared war against terrorism. All the accounts were freezed in the world and had pronounced that Al-Qaeda was a terrorist organization. US government had firmly announced to clean the world from terrorists. This war is called "war against terrorism". It was proclaimed that Osama Bin Laden and his companions was occupant of Taliban government. US invaded on Afghanistan to castigate the terrorist. US forces along with Britain, Germany and other countries with her back started heavy missile and air strike on Afghanistan at October 7, 2001. The war has caused large scale of entrance of Afghan refugees into Pakistan. This created a serious challenging situation in the country.

Mushraf drove the military in the Pakistan and work on US agenda as Bush address in his speech," the new Pakistani general, he's just been elected….not elected, this guy took over office"(Bush, 1999). Pakistan has served US foreign policies objective during the cold war and after that. Geopolitically Pakistan is a hub for US military and intelligence operations. As a neighbor country of Afghanistan, Pakistan gained world attention on war against terrorism. US preferred Pakistan for the purpose of logistics and intelligence support in Afghanistan. Pakistan provided all these supports to US and her allies on global war against terror in Afghanistan.

Ex-president Mushraf decided to join US without any vacillation. After the assault US government, as these were,' over flight rights, access to

Pakistani air, naval and land bases, crush the domestic elements who are in supporting of terrorism against Americans and its allies, end every logistics and diplomatic support to Talban" (Khan, 2009).

In 2002, Mushraf ordered a military operation in the tribal areas of Pakistan. This was the first military operation of the Pakistan Army on its homeland which resulted hundreds of civilians and arms forces casualties. In 2003, Pak-army killed several Al Qaeda suspects and captured more than 400 terrorist. While in 2004, Pakistan started a military operation on the US will in Waziristan and killed about 300 terrorist. These operations resulted chaos and antipathy in the mind of Pakistan's masses. Local tribal leaders stood against Pakistan's so called war on terror which generated immense problem for Pakistan's security forces. In 2005, Pakistan confirmed that it had captured more than 600 militant and round about 150 have been killed. In this operation Pakistan army sacrificed 200 soldiers. This proves the unremitting labours of Pakistan efforts in this war on terrorism. US government and media again alleged that Pakistan is secretly supporting Taliban (Khan, 2009). In 2006, seven terrorist attacks have been conducted inside Pakistan. Pakistan armed forces faced top extent of rebellion and insurgency in the country. Baitullah Mehsud in 2007 has spread its anti state and anti human activities with the help of his foreign advisors in FATA. Pakistan army launched its military operation Rah-e-Rast against these in insurgents. Pakistan forces defeated terrorist in this operation successfully. Pak-US Business Council Report (2009), calculated that Pakistan was the prime victim of terrorism and instability, and its economy has so for suffered directly or indirectly a gigantic failure of 35 billion dollars.

1.6   Pakistan Image in the West

Pakistan is a failed state it has been claimed by many western writers and in CIA reports. Western media and writers without realization of people and government's attitudes toward extremism and terrorism kept biased wordplay about the country and asserted that it is a hub of terrorism (Fair, 2005). Such arbitrated messages about war and terrorism obviously created diverse perception about Pakistan in the mind of US citizens (Vender, 2004). In fact US media supported their government policies and interests. MaChesney (2002) criticized that American media support its country policies. It is due to that US media provide protection to interest of ruling class in the country.

All the content generated in US media after the 9/11 were biased. CNN has produced biased news coverage on war against terrorism in different for the world as its US channel served (MeChesney, 2002). When any issue is more important to America, US media gives most importance to these issues. Sleem, (2005) describes it ,' US media protect and project national interest Vis-à-vis U.S. competing powers such as China and Russia. US media frames the negative image of South Asian countries in its contents (Poornananda, 1998). US media's framing of other country's image depends upon the degree of US interest in that country as well as US foreign policy (Siraj, 2010).

Besides sacrifices US urges Pakistan to "do more". US media as well as Obama administration blame that Pakistan is secretly sporting Taliban. US National Council and CIA predict that Pakistan will become failed state by 2015. These so called reports about Pakistan arises a question in the researcher mind to investigate the phenomena. US media has a strong influence on US foreign policy. As it proved that mass media is a powerful institution in constructing the public opinion.

1.7   Problem Statement

This study explores how the image of Pakistan was portrayed by the US media after the 9/11 terrorist incident and during the afghan war against terrorism. Given the significance of 9/11 to the American people and the American government, and the position of Pakistan in the fight against terror which come forward from this episode, this study investigate how the American media, focus to the various manipulate that result in journalists assigning meaning and significance to people and events framed Pakistan. As in 2009 altering of US administration indict Pakistan is not sincere on war against terrorism. US clearly insisted Pakistan "to do more" on war against terrorism. US media propagated that Pakistan is not serious on war against terror and supporting the terrorist organizations. Researcher tries to explore the phenomenon to find out the reality.

1.8   Objectives of study

The major objectives of the study are as follows
1.   To examine the portrayal of U S press toward Pakistan regarding the war against terrorism.
2.   To know about the image of Pakistan in the U S press in building the perception of the world about Pakistan.
3. To identify the direction of image of Pakistan economic, political and military issues on the both magazines.

1.9   Limitation of the Study

1.   The present study tries to focus on the articles related about the

economic, political and military issues of Pakistan. It does not take into account the advertisements and other sections of the magazines for the purpose of study.

2.   The above mentioned study covers two leading US magazines. Time and Newsweek these magazines selected due to vast readership.

3.   The 128 articles of both magazines from July, 2009 to December, 2009 were analyzed for the purpose of study.

1.10   Scope and Significance of the Study

The role of press has been acknowledged throughout the world. We know that the press is the fourth pillar of the state. It plays a fundamental function in the societies in shaping and moulding the public opinion. Pakistan and America have close relation on war against terror. U.S. supports Pakistan in fighting poverty, educational and military development. This study focuses at understanding each other feeling in the media coverage. This study aims to investigate the nature and treatment of the American print media about Pakistan's image by the US news magazines. This research will be help full for the student of mass media and the international relations who want to know about the image of Pakistan in the US press. It will also offer the adequate knowledge for the researcher, policies makers, journalists and the ambassador of the both countries.

1.11   Research Question

Q. What image of Pakistan, the US magazines portray?

1.12   Hypothesis

H: Most of the coverage given by the US magazines after 9/11 portrays the negative image of Pakistan.

1.13   Methodology

This study aims to examine the portrayal of Pakistan by US press. The universe of the present study is leading news magazines of US. Online study with the combination of the hard copies of both magazines will be held for the purpose of research. These two magazines Newsweek and Time are the universe of the study. The said magazines are selected because of largest wide circulation. The study will contain 128 articles of both magazines in the time period of 1st July, 2009 to 31th December, 2009. A qualitative research approach was adopted for the purpose of study using the content analysis method. The Unit of analysis was article related to Pakistan of the both magazines.

1.13.1 Research Design

The study conducted following steps:
1. Measuring the coverage of article related to Pakistan published in both magazines.
2. Indentified the coverage devoted in each magazine positive, negative and neutral.
3. Calculating the ratio of coverage devoted in each of these magazines and an average for the total period of study.
4. Analyzing and comparing the results from the study.

.

2 LITERATURE REVIEW

2.1 Chronological View of Pak – US Relations

The history of Pak-US relations is spread over more than last three decades. These three decades show many ups and downs between the relations of two countries. Pak-US relations started when Paul Alling, a US diplomat arrived Karachi. After that, in 1950 first Prime Minster of Pakistan visited America. That was the formal initiate of relationship between the two countries. As we examine the history of these relations we come to know that relationship of US with India was balanced while Pak-US relation in the region was unbalanced (Khan, 2010).

We can divide this relationship into three different periods. First period is cold war period, second is period of crisis after cold war from 1990 to2000 and third is after the 9/11 era. Pakistan has sustained good relation in the tenure period of Eisenhower, Nixon and Reagan. Whereas period of Kennedy, Johnson, Carter, Bush senior, and Clinton, was more critical and chill (Khan, 2010).

Soviet Union had started to expand its interest toward the Indian Ocean and the Persian Gulf. It made the most critical situation in the region. Revolution of Iran and Russian's attack on Afghanistan in 1979 put Pakistan to gained more attention of the world as well as Washington. A security agreement laid down between America and Pakistan for strategic cooperation in 1959 (Jameel, 2010).US think tank and policy maker consider Pakistan as failed state but the incident of 9/11 again increase the geo strategic position of Pakistan. Sameea (2007) describes it as:

"The growing consensus among American policymakers and lawmakers was that Pakistan was not only losing its strategic importance to the United States; it was also becoming an unreliable failed state. That perception was partly transformed after September 11, when Pakistan became a critical theater in the U.S. effort to take the fight to the terrorists."

Former prime Minister of Pakistan M.A. Bogra joined a "mutual defense assistance program" (Rasool, 2010) with Eisenhower Former President of America. Later Pakistan joined the West through signing two defense pacts, like the South East Asian Treaty Organization (SEATO) and Central Treaty Organization (CENTO). These two pacts were signed behind the different motives of the both countries. US joined these pacts because he required a military base in south Asia against Soviet Union. But Pakistan joined these pacts as he was looking for a powerful friend against Russia which was an ally of India. As the results of that pacts Pakistan obtained funding and some military aid from 1953 to 1961 (Rasool, 2010). Khan (2010) said:

"After World War II, containment of Soviet Union was on top of the US agenda. Geographically and strategically Pakistan fitted into the US scheme of encirclement, intelligence gathering, and preventing Communist expansion into West and South Asia"

Pak-US relations in the period of 2001 to the beginning of 2009 have mostly been suspicious. In the cold war era, Pakistan provided full cooperation and assistance to US and the Western world. Pakistan supported the western promoted Jihad against Russian invasion in Afghanistan. This support of Jihad affected the society of Pakistan very badly. Pakistan faced the problems of more than two million Afghan refugees. It dragged the Pakistan into the religious extremism, drug culture and proliferation of weapons. Pakistan has suffered very destructive situation and torment after the end of cold war. At the end of cold war US changed its policies toward Pakistan. The immediate and basic cause of differences between two countries was nuclear program of Pakistan. US officials, Ambassadors and policy maker tried to persuade Pakistan to avoid attaining the nuclear power. James Buckley in November12, 1981,"Undersecretary of State demonstrated as before the Senate Foreign Relations Committee", that:

"We believe that a program of support which provides Pakistan with a continuing relationship with a significant security partner and enhances its sense of security may help remove the principal underlying incentive for the acquisition of a nuclear weapons capability. With such a relationship in place we are hopeful that over time we will be able to persuade Pakistan that the pursuant of a weapons capability is neither necessary to its security nor in its broader interest as an important member of the world community."

US ministers and secretaries of state always tried to forbid Pakistan to never attain nuclear technology. In November 1, 1983, Richard Kennedy, demonstrated as, before two House subcommittees:

"By helping friendly nations to address legitimate security concerns, we seek to reduce incentives for the acquisition of nuclear weapons. The provision of security assistance and the sale of military equipment can be major components of efforts along these lines. Development of security ties to the U.S. can strengthen a country's confidence in its ability to defend itself without nuclear weapons. At the same time, the existence of such a relationship enhances our credibility when we seek to persuade that country to forego [sic] nuclear arms . . . We believe that strengthening Pakistan's conventional military capability serves a number of important U.S. interests, including non-proliferation. At the same time, we have made clear to the government of Pakistan that efforts to acquire nuclear explosives would jeopardize our security assistance program."

In 1992, US imposed military and economic sanction on Pakistan through the Pressler Amendment. This amendment made only for one country on the issue of nuclear technology. In fact main reason to impose these laws was to hold back the military equipment worth of $1.2 billion which was paid by Pakistan (Khan, 2010).

It is the reality that policies of US are altered according to its national interest. Its ally of some decades may be its foe in the next year and recompensation of their sacrifice will not entertain. As Kissinger pointed out that; in international politics "there are neither permanent friends nor permanent foes of a state" (cited in Khan, 2010). When we have to take an over view of the Pak-US relations before the incident of 9/11 we can indentify many ups and downs between the two countries.

In 1965, India attacked Pakistan, at that time of trouble US left Pakistan alone and stopped the military support. Ayaz Ahmed Khan (2010) gives details that:

"But the US played no role, and remained neutral during the 1965 Indo-Pak war. Washington expressed anger that US weapons meant for fighting the Soviet Union were used against India. Supplies of US weapons and spares were stopped and close ally Pakistan was suddenly left high and dry.........................While America let Pakistan down in its hour of need, Peoples Republic of China emerged as a solid pillar of support, and offered weapons with technology. It became clear that the United States is not a reliable friend of Pakistan. In 1965 Washington ignored Indian aggression on Pakistan"

Later on freedom of Bangladesh position of US was skewed toward Pakistan. After that when Pakistan become the Nuclear power in 1998 US imposed sanctions against Pakistan. In 1999 when military General Pervez Musharraf overthrew the political government of Nawaz Sharif, government of US was vehemently criticized it (*Siraj, and Ramaprasad, 2007*).

The relations with US on war against terrorism resulted Pakistan unstable and internal terrorism. Historical view of Pak-US relation present the diversity in the relations between two countries. As Saeed (2007) said that:

" Osama Bin Laden with his organization Al Qaida was suspected to have their base in Afghanistan and Taliban government was their supporter. Due to the geographical proximity of Pakistan with Afghanistan, and a day before 9/11 Pakistan was staunch supporter of Taliban. It was observed that Pakistan had to face some difficult days ahead. After the stunning attacks of September 11, 2001 US started to contour his new strategy to counter the situation. President G.W Bush declared the struggle between good versus evil."

After the horrible attacks of 9/11, US its allies once again saw Pakistan as a front-line state in the war against Al-Qaeda. Thus 9/11 opens another opportunity for both countries to work closely. As Pakistan has an open threat from US to join or ready for consequences. Robert Nolan reported, "American officials had told Musharraf's government that Washington would use every lever short of war to punish Pakistan unless it cooperated". President Musharraf at that time endowed with extensive support to America. His positive response exceeded expectation (Amir, 2001). Pakistan hoped that through US support he will achieved the economic growth, safeguard its "strategic nuclear and missile assets," and Kashmir dispute will be resolve (Musharraf, 2001). But resolution of these problems was seemed as illusions. As Baloch (2007) noted that,

"Islamabad was pressurized to alter its national course on Kashmir, withdraw its support from freedom movement in Kashmir, and declare some of the echelons of the freedom movement as terrorist organization, banning their operation at its soil. Besides, the few voices for government support, the overall public reaction to Pakistan's U turns on its long tested policies under U.S. pressure was largely skeptical. Pakistan cooperation with the United States included; granting logistics facilities, sharing intelligence, and capturing and handing over al-Qaida suspects, sealing off its western border and made two naval bases, three air force bases, and its airspace available to the U.S. military."

Through the historical background we conclude that mutual relations between US and Pakistan are grounded on convergence of common interests periodically. In the cold war Pakistan was an important country for US and after that it turned off his policies, and after 9/11 once again Pakistan has importance for america.US support military dictator for his national interest not for Pakistan prosperity.

2.2 Foreign Policies of US toward Pakistan

Pakistan and America experience very close relations from the last 60 years. These relations bound the interests of both countries. US policies toward Pakistan are altering according to the international state of affairs. Historically US support the military rulers for its national interest and also appreciate to the struggle for democracy. Geo-strategic position of Pakistan enhances the importance of Pakistan for West and America. With countering terrorism and Al-Qaeda in Afghanistan it is not possible to US to fight with them without the help of Pakistan. Incident of 9/11, made an opportunity for President Bush to eradicate the global terrorism from the world. Pakistan was placed strategically very important state offense against terrorism to al-Qaeda in Bush agenda. US policies had many interest in Pakistan. This covered wide range of issues including nuclear program of Pakistan, war against terrorism and missile proliferation. The other concerns of US policies are human rights, democracy, economic reforms and counter to narcotics trafficking. In Musharraf regime US started aid to Pakistan. Kronstadt (2005) note as:

"Direct assistance programs include aid for health, education, food, democracy promotion, child labor elimination, counter-narcotics, border security and law enforcement, as well as trade preference benefits. The United States also supports grant, loan, and debt rescheduling programs for Pakistan by the various major international financial institutions."

Secretary Clinton (2009) said, "If Pakistan becomes more financially unstable, it increases the danger that we will face from the threat by the extremists to the Pakistan Government." There are several reasons behind the stability of Pakistan, for the US foreign policy interest. Martin and Kronstadt (2009) defined it as:

"There is an opportunity for the United States to demonstrate its support for Pakistan by providing a portion of the $2 billion - $7 billion Pakistan will likely still need to cover its capital shortfall. Others think that the United States should condition additional aid on Pakistan increasing its commitment to combat Islamist militancy along its border with Afghanistan."

Bark Obama addressed to 'Meet the Press' (2008) that:

"...we need a strategic partnership with all the parties in the region-- Pakistan and India and the Afghan government--to stamp out the kind of militant, violent, terrorist extremists that have set up base camps and that are operating in ways that threaten the security of everybody in the international community. And, as I've said before, we can't continue to look at Afghanistan in isolation."

Bark Obama administration once take an overview to its policies toward Pakistan and war against terrorism. US publically announced that Pakistan failed to deal with terrorist. Pakistan is also going to in a destructive stride faced from terrorist. Kfir (2009) noted that,

"The terrorists within Pakistan's borders are not simply enemies of America or Afghanistan--they are a grave and urgent danger to the people of Pakistan. Al Qaeda and other violent extremists have killed several thousand Pakistanis since 9/11. They have killed many Pakistani soldiers and police. They assassinated Benazir Bhutto. They have blown up buildings, derailed foreign investment, and threatened the stability of the state. Make no mistake: al Qaeda and its extremist allies are a cancer that risks killing Pakistan from within."

The other significant decision of US is the stability of democracy and political system in Pakistan. Economic development and the social sector reforms can reduce the activity of terrorist. Obama administration (Kfir, 2009) pointed that, "by improving the political situation--a codeword for democracy promotion--Pakistan could successfully deal with its internal and external terrorist problem."

In 2009, Kerry Lugar bill introduced which is a new step of US policies toward Pakistan. This Act emphasized on the failing situation in Pakistan. It shows the endless commitment of the US to Pakistan (Kfir, 2009). This bill provides a large amount financial aid to meet the new tide of terrorism in the country. Kfir (2009) wrote;

"The goals of the act are also for Pakistan to support and consolidate democracy and the rule of law in the country. Second, the act pledges to help Pakistan establish the conditions conducive for stability, with references made to economic security. Third, the legislation seeks to provide Pakistan with the means to prevent and combat the usage of its territory for terrorist camps. This includes helping the Pakistanis develop the tools for improving coordination and cooperation among the military, paramilitary, and police action against terrorists. That is, the act recognizes that each branch operates against terrorists in Pakistan, but far too often, there is a failure to communicate between the branches, which undermine the counterterrorism efforts. Finally, the Kerry-Lugar Act hopes to improve relations between Pakistan and the United States, especially as Kerry and Lugar noted that the United States is not widely esteemed in Pakistan."

2.3 Incident of 9/11 and Pakistan

The terrorist attacks on World Trade Centre have spectator that these incidents extremely affected Pakistan's national solidity and economic condition. After the attacks of 9/11 once again Pakistan has become the front-line state in the war against terrorism. US willing to invasion at

Afghanistan, but Afghanistan was a landlocked country so US required airspaces and air bases for logistics support form neighbour countries. US started talk with Turkmenistan, Uzbekistan and Tajikistan for support but its first priority was to Pakistan's support for invasion. Because most of the US supplies on ships route was possible through the Indian Ocean. Pakistan was a viable ally for America for assault. In the war against terrorism Washington asked Pakistan to decide in the 24 hour, whether "it would be on America's side or not (Musharraf, 2007)". Collins (2008) explain it that US administration,

" made it clear to Pakistan that it wanted intelligence support, the use of Pakistan's airspace, and logistical support.   Although the U.S. never directly threatened the use of force, U.S. officials threatened to add Pakistan to a State Department list of seven terrorist-sponsoring nations which would portend the possibility of U.S. force.   According to one high-ranking official at U.S. Embassy in Islamabad, President Musharraf was told to either abandon support of Taliban or be prepared to be treated like the Taliban".

Next day on September 13, 2001, President General Pervaiz Musharraf showed green signal to US, to joining international coalition against terrorism (Dawn, 2001). On September 19, 2001, after the higher official meeting President of Pakistan General Pervaiz Musharraf addressed the nation on television and clarified,

"We in Pakistan are facing a very critical situation. Perhaps as critical as the events in 1971. If we make the wrong decisions our vital interests will be harmed, our critical concerns are our sovereignty, second our economy, third our strategic assets, (nuclear, missiles) and fourth our Kashmir cause. All four will be harmed. If we make these decisions they must be according to Islam. It is not the question of bravery or cowardice. But bravery without thinking is stupidity. We have to save our interests. Pakistan comes first everything else is secondary."

Pakistan has cooperated with US through providing logistics facilities, capturing al-Qaida suspects and sharing of intelligence. Pakistan has closed up its western border. It also grants two naval bases and three air force basis to US military (9/11 Commission Report). United States has granted Pakistan equaling $1 billion and exempt $ 1 billion in debt. In 2003, United States also announced a five year aid package of $3 billion for Pakistan. US provided $2.63 billion direct aid between 2002 and 2005 (Kronstadt, 2006). Moreover both countries signed an agreement on trade and investment. According to Baloch (2007) an arms-sale package is also approved by the United States,

"Package that includes purchase of P3C Orion aircraft, surveillance radars, helicopters and radio communication system in order to improve Pakistan capacity to support U.S led forces in War on Terrorism. Besides, offering F-16 fighter jets to refurbish its Air Force, Pakistan has been declared to be a major non- NATO ally of the United States."

US assistance to Pakistan has not focus on strengthen Pakistan's internal stability. Its primary objective was to achieve a specific goal in counter terrorism in the country western border and in Afghanistan. It was a political stipulated assistance, and a reward of Mushraf's regime cooperation to US on counter terrorism. The 9/11 commissioners deducible that U.S. assistance had not, "moved sufficiently beyond in this security assistance to include significant funding for education efforts." (Thomas, 2005). Cohen, (2007) explain it as,

" In this way, very little **is** unique about the current U.S.-Pakistani relationship. It is history repeating itself, resembling the relationship in the 1980s when the United States established a quid pro quo with General Muhammad Zia-ul-Haq to help fight the Soviets. Any efforts by U.S. officials to alter the terms of the arrangements to focus on internal reforms would prompt Zia's reply, "Sir, what you are proposing is 11 neither part of the quid nor the quo."

A senior level Triparties Commission is established among Pakistan, Afghanistan and NATO. Through that military supply and training on how to use US weapons against terrorist is shared.

2.4   Drone Attacks inside Pakistan

Drone attacks inside the Pakistan badly impede the war against terrorism. Actually these attacks killed civilians more than targeted Talban. These civilian's causalities increase the insurgency in the tribal areas. Under US administration these attacks were called a part of war against terrorism. These attacked were started under the Bush administration and have continued under the Bark Obama presidency. The Washington post reported on October 4, 2008 that Pakistan government has a secret deal with US to permitting Drone attacks. But Pakistan foreign minister Shah Mehmood Qureshi denied it. Obama government secretly permitted CIA to carry out more drone attacks in Pakistan.

Drone attacks have been initiated to target the Al-Qaeda. Los Angeles Time reported it as," the CIA received secret permission to attack a wide range of target, including militant whose name are not known" (Auken, 2010). According to Abbot (2010) that Pakistan "residents interviewed by the Associated Press in Pakistan's North Waziristan tribal area, the site of a majority of the strikes since the program began in 2004, said they believe almost all of the victims are innocent civilians." Wikipedia (2010) explain it that there are 179 attacks from 2004 to October9, 2010 and 1825 deaths where majority of civilians deaths recorded.

3 THEORATICAL FRAMEWORK

This study attempted to understand the image of Pakistan in the US magazines and how it frames the Pakistan in its articles. Theory means an attempt to explaining a particular phenomenon. It is as Kaplan (1964) explains "a way of making sense of a disturbing situation" (p.295).

There are many theories available in the literature regarding mass media which developed by many scholars. The researcher required the support of agenda setting theory and framing theory for this particular research. The researcher selects the theory of framing and agenda setting theory for this study which is more suitable for this study.

2.6 Agenda Setting Theory

The origin of the idea of agenda setting has its roots from an old book, Public Opinion written by Lippmann (1922). In this book Lippmann said that "The World Outside and the Pictures in Our Heads." It is the media which inform us about the world according to his on perspective. Mass media present the picture of the world in the audience mind Lippmann (1922) and people not think that what they like to think. But what media feed them they start to thinking about that issue or the story.

In the news media people did not access to the reality. They can only see the reflection of the reality and subsequently they start thinking about the world on the basis of that reflection. That information or reality presented by the news media mostly deficient or distorted. Riaz (2008) explore it,

"There is another dimension of the agenda-setting role of media. Each of the objects portrayed by media has numerous attributes, and these attributes open doors for another agenda. Just like things, the attributes of these things vary in salience. The selection of things for attention and the selection of attributes is simultaneously powerful agenda setting roles. News media agenda and its daily set of objects provide different aspects that media people and then general public think about each object. These perspectives of the news media draw attention of their audience to certain attributes and keep them away from others."

An empirical study was conduct by two researcher McCombs & Shaw (1972) to investigate the idea that news media organization influence the perception of the individuals. According to Tankard (1991) "Agenda-setting is one of the possible way that the mass media can have an effect on the public". In the last decade media has raised its importance by reporting the crisis of the world. Entman (2000) point out that US media, "seem to provide the most consistently interventionist elite voices in post-Cold War America". Agenda setting research begin with paying attention on "the relationship between media coverage of issues and perceptions of issue importance among the general public" (Salmon, 2003). Dunaway, et.all. (2007) explore it,

"Agenda setting describes the process by which the news media shows the public what is important by giving more salience to certain events and issues more than other issues. Because of increased media attention, Specific issues are more salient in the minds of citizens. As a result, the public perceives those issues which receive the majority of media coverage to be the ones of greatest importance"

With the advent of sophisticated means of measuring the relationship between mass media and public has become the development of opening theoretical concept, which state media not only inform us but also influence us as to what is important to know. In other words, media create an agenda for our thoughts and influence us in what seems important. McCombs and Shaw (2002) wrote that,

"The agenda-setting function of mass communication clearly falls in this new tradition of cognitive outcomes of mass communication. Perhaps more than any other aspect of our environment, the political arena—all those issues and persons about whom we hold opinions and knowledge is second-hand reality. Especially, in national politics, we have little personal or direct contact. Our knowledge comes primarily from the mass media. For the most part, we know only those aspects of national politics considered newsworthy enough for transmission through the mass media." p.5

2.7 Priming Theory

Several studies proved that there were powerful media effects which work beyond the agenda setting. At the first time Iyengar, Peters, and Kinder (1982) explore these dimensions as "priming effect". It can be defined that, "process in which the media attend to some issues and not others and thereby alter the standards by which people evaluate election candidates" (MTSU32, 2009). Theory made assumptions that in political maters masses do not have adequate knowledge of political matters and at the time of decisions on political issues like in election they depend on the media for deciding about political matters. Morgan (2010) explained it as,

The strength of these relationships political views is determined by semantic associations between concepts in memory and the frequency with which the links have been used".

Priming founded on media effects research during an experiment of agenda setting research by Iyengar, Peters, and Kinder (1982). This study was conduct on T.V. news coverage of three issues like pollution, defense and inflation. They compared it with the perceived control groups of people and measure rating of President Carter's presentation on these issues. They resulted that media ignore some issue to exposing other and formulate the public opinion according to its depicted standards. These standards called "Priming". Kempf (2002) explains that there are three steps exist in priming when mass media not expose the society outlook but plays an "active role in stimulating the process of conflict escalation beyond its actual level" (p. 70). Step first is happened earlier than violence break out. The media hold attention or offer ordinary on clash issues even violence has not broken out (Kempf). According to Kempf the second step is "when journalists take notice of a conflict, finally, they often rush to antagonistic conclusions without adequate analysis of the conflict constellation" (p. 70). The third step present that media men have close relations with the elite who supply them that information (Kempf). These way journalists propagate and set agenda about that for their audience. Agenda setting and Priming theories has proved that news media was able to influence on the opinion of the public. Through this way news media has a strong effect on audience to direct their attitude (Tankard, 1997).

2.8   Framing Theory

During the setting of agenda media sometimes prefer to sustain or reject information to achieve specific reactions from the public. A key ingredient in agenda setting is framing the story. Framing is an analyzing method which developed by social psychologists (Goffman, 1974; Entamn, 1991; Gitlin, 1980) that how news media defined the issues of public interest. Goffman's, (1974) define framing as "the principles of organization, which govern social events" (p. 232).

Framing is the way the media "chooses to shape the presentation of an issue" (Jasperson, et. all, 1998). Gamson and Modigliani (1987) defined framing as a "central organizing idea" or "story line" that gives meaning to any event. Neuman et al. (1992). defined news frames as "conceptual tools" that news media apply and audiences rely on "to convey, interpret, and evaluate information" (p.60). For example, In war on Iraq media move toward their stories through plenty of news stories of its interest. Dillard, Solomon, & Samp (1996) describes framing as; "frames are the lenses through which social reality is viewed". Chong and Druckman, (2007) explained it as,

"But politics is typically competitive, fought between parties or ideological factions, and issues that are debated are framed in opposing terms. Individuals receive multiple frames with varying frequencies. In one of the few experiments that has tested the effect of simultaneous exposure to opposing frames".

Gitlin (1980) defines media frames as, "persistent patterns of cognition, interpretation, and presentation of selection, emphasis, and exclusion, by which symbol-handlers routinely organize discourse, whether verbal or visual". Framing is a term used in mass communication means that how any event is portrayed in any article or story. The central organizing idea of any issue which makes a sense is called framing (Gamson, 1989, p. 157; Gamson and Modigliani, 1987, p. 43). Mann (1999) argued that the media coverage of international affairs often reporting as;

"reporters do not always get the story right; neither do their editors and publishers. This is especially the case when they report about distant lands and unfamiliar cultures...the readers, who are already conditioned by the prevalent stereotypes, accept the misleading stories as true and react accordingly. The consequences can be disastrous media effects are enhanced when the information conveyed in stories in unfamiliar to audience and cannot be readily verified through their personal experiences or competing stories. This is why foreign affairs reporting demands the attention of experienced, highly skilled, and well informed reporters" (p. 102).

Entman (1993) journalist often build framing "select some aspects of a perceived reality and make them more salient in a communicating text, in such a way as to promote a particular problem definition, causal interpretation, moral evaluation, and/or treatment recommendation for the item described" (p. 56). Biased involvement of the media man in an issue is also a framing (Tuchman, 1978). Tiung and Hasim (2009) described that,

"Framing and priority in the mass media are decisive role agenda which refers to mass media capacity in choosing and stresses some particular issue until it becomes important to the people and consequently affect public opinions. Framing refers to the way a certain media carry out restrictions towards a certain issue to be put before the society. Framing influences the way how the news will be presented to the people through agenda setting and not only can it explain what is being thought and also to explain how to think about the issue. Focus will be given towards how a hot issue will be carried out. The main title will be emphasized because it is believed that it can have a great influence and overall, it will help to make the news objective and perfect". p.411

Media coverage mostly favored the elite class and promotes their opinion. This way media frames seemed very powerful in society. They work as social forces that mold the public opinion and promote the ideology Gitlin (1980). Hackett (1984) explain on Gitlin's definition of media frames and he disagrees to that, "the ideology provides a framework through which events are presented" (Hackett, 1984 cited in Mughees, 1993, p. 66).

The countries where journalist enjoy the rights of freedom of expression they used self imposed restriction on themselves. While they frame reality according to their on perception and think that they do that for the best interest of their media organization (Bourdieu, 1998 cited in Saleem, 2007). Media frames including attractive words, metaphors, phrases etc also help to determine the "tone" of media coverage of an event or issue (Saleem, 2007). Salmon, Post and Christensen, (2003) explains framing as,

"The plan and strategy of media advocacy mirror the news Values of news organizations. Thus, media advocates are trained in this approach to conceptualize their audience as media gatekeepers/decision makers as well as members of the general public, and to frame their stories accordingly."

News media framing is a solemn matter now a day as it is part of the agenda-setting process. Through framing media influences on the opinion of the audience. It develops the public opinion about an issue either positively or negatively. Kerr (2002) argues that frames are capable of generating social effects when encoded in specific phrases, particularly once the phrase is widely accepted. Thus, through news framing, journalists can play a powerful role in determining success or failure, for example, of social movements. In Edelrhan's, (1993) words, the media's framing means that,

"The character, causes, and consequences of any phenomenon become radically different as changes are made in what is prominently displayed, what is repressed, and especially in how observations are classified. Far from being stable, the social world is ... a kaleido-scope of potential realities, any of which can be readily evoked by altering the ways in which observations are framed and categorized. Because alternative categorizations win support for specific political beliefs and policies, classification schemes are central to political maneuver and political persuasion"

News media framing is a solemn matter now a day as it is part of the agenda-setting process. Through framing media influences on the opinion of the audience. It develops the public opinion about any issue either positively or negatively.

2.9 Gate Keeping Theory

In journalism and mass media gatekeeping means to filter any information for broadcasting or publishing purpose. Internal decision of media men's to relaying or withholding some information to audience or public. Founder of this theory was Kurt Lewin (1890-1947). Gatekeeping has taken place at all level of the mass media institutions. Reporter select the source and collection of information what to forward to his media, editors and producers decide on what to print or broadcast to masses. As McQuail (1994) explains,

"the gatekeeping concept, despite its usefulness and its potential for dealing with many different situations, has a built-in limitation in its implication that news arrives in ready-made and unproblematic event-story form at the 'gates' of the media, where it is either admitted or excluded. The gatekeeping framework is largely based on the assumption ... that there is a given, finite, knowable reality of events in the 'real world', from which it is the task of the media to select according to appropriate criteria of representativeness or relevance." p.214

Now a day's world shrunk its boundaries and become the global village. Mass earns the way of living through media exposures. But the media is not able to expose them all information about the world. It provides the selective message and information to its audience. Media receives thousands messages and news but publish the selective information. This way media play the role of gatekeeper in filtering the news for public.

"The very recent phenomenon of 'embedded journalism' can also be called as one of the products of the gatekeeping theory. Usually, this phenomenon is used by the media organizations during wartime when they are 28 allowed only to record and show some selected areas and pictures desired by the authorities. They are not at all allowed to report any side of the picture against the policy of the defence authorities by whom they are paid. Although the phenomenon exists for a long time in different shapes, but it got famous during the recent Iraq war when the US military used media to show the one-sided picture of the Iraq war. The reporters are hired to write their news stories in a desired way because they are highly paid and facilitated by the authorities. For example they may be asked by the military officers to print the pictures of their success and not the pictures of their defeat or death of their soldiers". p 27-28

Gatekepping is mostly adopted by the media in controlling the information. Actually we are also play the role of gatekeeper in our daily life in speaking, listing and watching. We try to listen our selective radio stations and watch our favourt TV channels it is the gatekeeping.

4 RESEARCH DESIGN AND METHODOLOGY

This chapter expresses the research methodology working in this study. In this chapter researcher focus on methodologies and the process through this research is concluded. This research intends to look into Pakistan's representation in US leading news magazines. Whether these magazines portray image of Pakistan positive or negative? Researcher carries out the content analysis of US leading news magazines. Data is collected from primary sources.

3.1 Research Design in Social Sciences

Frey, Botan and Gary L. Kreps (2000) describes that research is "The form of disciplined inquiry that involves studying something in a planned manner and reporting it so that other inquirers can potentially replicate the process if they chose." Thyer (1993) explain it as;

"A traditional research design is a blueprint or detailed for how a research study is to be completed—operationalizing variables so they can be measured, selecting a sample of interest to study, collecting data to be used as a basis for testing hypotheses, and analyzing the results."

Research process describes relationship between the research purpose and process of research. A valid study conducts an appropriate methodology and a suitable tool for data collection (Mouton, 2001). Kerlinger (1986) defined it:

"A research design is a plan, structure and strategy of investigation so conceived as to obtain answer to research questions or problems. The plan is the complete scheme or program of the research. It includes an outline of what the investigator will do from writing the hypotheses and their operational implications to the final analysis of data."

Basically there are two approaches that are used in gathering the data, namely qualitative and quantitative approaches. Researcher adopt the technique of content analysis in this research.

3.2   Universe of the Study

Universe of this study is US leading news magazines. Online study with combination of the hard copies of both magazines was calculated for the purpose of this research. These magazines have the largest wide circulation in the US as well in the world.

3.2.1   Sampling Method and Sample Size

This part of the study describes the sampling methods and how it chosen from the population. Time and Newsweek are the U.S. leading news magazines. Time is the first largest news magazine in the U.S. Its circulation was 3,360,135 in 2008 (Wikipedia, 2009). Newsweek is a US based weekly news magazine. It is the second largest news magazine in the U.S "which target elite audience". Its circulation was 2,720,034 in the 2008 (Wikipedia, 2009).

They have large distribution in the United State and throughout the world. On the basis of wide circulation both magazines were selected for the study. Both magazines of six month from July 2009 to December 2009 were selected for this research. The entire articles related to Pakistan economic, politics and military issues published in both magazines are the sample size of the study.

3.3   Research Process

It describes the process of research and procedure which researcher follow in this study. Researcher follows the following process;

3.3.1   Content Analysis

In qualitative research Content analysis is a valuable technique. It is a toll for analyzing the message of some certain communicator. It has been defined as the: "objective, systematic, and quantitative description" (Budd, Thorp, & Donohew, 1967, p.3). It can be defined that systemic approaches to abbreviate various words or sentences into small categories. These categorized should be unambiguous and clear based on coding rules (Berelson, 1952). Through this way researcher put wide range of data into the small. It can be defined as, "content analysis research is motivated by the search for techniques to infer from symbolic data what would be either too costly, no longer possible, or too obtrusive by the use of other techniques" (Krippendorff, 1980). Furthermore, content analyses offer an experimental foundation for monitoring modification in public opinion. As sum up by Starosta (1984),

"Content analysis translates frequency of occurrence of certain symbols into summary judgments and comparisons of content of the discourse... whatever "means" will presumably take up space and/or time; hence, the greater that space and/or time, the greater the meaning's significance."

In this research Content of the two US leading news magazines, Newsweek and Time will be analyzed for this study. Researcher selects these magazines due to wide circulation of both in US as well as the whole World. These magazines had powerful effect on the global issues. The content analysis of the issues related to the economics, politics and military of Pakistan were analyzed.

3.3.2 Types of Content Analysis

Basically there are two types of content analysis:
a) Qualitative
b) Quantitative

Qualitative approach is based in interpretive social sciences paradigm. Qualitative method is the tool to understanding the human experience, behavior, attitude and their belief. It explained as, "Qualitative methodology is legitimate and valuable, possessing distinctive characteristics that make it ideal for many types of investigations" (NOVA, 2000). Researcher adopts the method of content analysis which is appropriate for this research. In qualitative analysis researcher has focus on to know the number or frequency of similar context.

A combination of qualitative and quantitative analysis has offered the better understanding of research question. Findings of quantitative analysis were followed by qualitative analysis. In this study basic categories of context were recognized. These categories were based on articles of Newsweek and Time magazines. For the purpose of qualitative analysis researcher read the whole material many time for the accuracy of findings. For the classification of the text researcher has categorized the data into four categories. Similarity of issues were label into a category which given a specific name.

3.4 Construction of the Categories

Floger (1984) describes it as, "to which the coding system is logically consistent and the categories clearly defined" p.137. Potter et al. (1999) defined it that, "The designer of content analysis develops a coding scheme that consists of rules that tells coders how to put their observations into the correct data categories" p.266. For the purpose of creating these categories researcher focus on the objective of the study and then distribute the data into the manageable categories. Newsweek and the Time magazines were the area of study. In these news magazines article related to Pakistan has been categorized into four categories. These categories are as;

1. Article Related to Terrorism
2. Article Related to Politics and Economy of Pakistan
3. Article Related to Pakistan Military Operations
4. Miscellaneous

All these categories are described as;

Article Related to Terrorism

All articles based on terrorism, bomb blast, suicide bombing, activities of terrorist organizations, terrorist training camps, and support to terrorism in Pakistan were categorized in terrorism.

Article Related to Politics and Economy of Pakistan

All the articles presenting Pakistan economic conditions, political development, Pakistan's foreign relations and restoration of democracy are categorized in this category.

Article Related to Pakistan Military Operations

All the articles based on Pakistan military operations and Pakistan army role on war against terrorism. All the achievements of Pakistan's military like capturing the terrorist and destroying their net work and other military forces related activities in Pakistan are categorized in this category.

Miscellaneous

Article based on presenting the women's condition, judiciary crisis, culture, religious harmony and minorities condition in Pakistan. The articles which were not falling into one of above category but have the significance are categorized in this category.

3.4.1   Quantitative Part of Analysis

Six month of the study of Time and Newsweek was conducted for the purpose of investigating the image of Pakistan. Numbers of the articles of both magazines were counted for study from 1st July to 31th December, 2009. It counts the articles related to Pakistan on categories based and their directions separately.

3.4.2   Qualitative Part of Content Analysis

For exploring the image of Pakistan Time and Newsweek of six month were studied. All the articles relate to Pakistan published in both magazines were examined carefully. Whole the magazines of selected time period were scanned and articles related to Pakistan were read thoroughly. Relevant material was gathered, a frame was developed and directions were identified. In this study unit of coding was paragraphs of the articles. After coding of the paragraphs directions of articles were identified to examine the image of Pakistan.

3.5   Quality and Direction of the Contents

There are three types of slant paragraphs which indicate there directions as positive are favorable, those indicate negative are unfavorable and those which had no direction were coded as neutral. When the percentage of positive slant of paragraphs was increased on the negative slant of paragraphs, that article was considered as favorable. And where the ratio of negative slant paragraphs increased that article was considered unfavorable. Articles which had equal ratio were coded neutral.

Favorable (+)

Each paragraph of the article was coded in term of slant paragraph which indicate positive change and development in war on terrorism, portrays Pakistan as a friend country of US, nuclear non proliferation, hand over the terrorist to us, religious harmony, helping investigative agencies and protection of US citizen, economic development, art and culture were coded as favorable or positive.

Unfavorable (-)

On the other hand, paragraph which present Pakistan reluctant to cooperation, provide support to terrorist, sympathizing with the Taliban, nuclear proliferation, religious dissonance, terrorist infiltration into Afghanistan from Pakistan's border, lawlessness, fiscal and societal turmoil were coded as negative.

Neutral (o)

Paragraphs which had not any direction on image of Pakistan were coded as neutral.

5 ANALYSIS OF DATA

This chapter contains two parts which analysis the findings of research.

Part One

In the first portion quantitative results of data are analyzed, that simultaneously hold the directions of the articles on the basis of their categories. Following alphabetic are used to present the categories for the purpose of coding.

N   **= Number of Articles Related to Pakistan**

A   = Article Related to Terrorism

B   = Article Related to Politics and Economy

C   = Article Related to Pakistan Military Operations

D   = Miscellaneous

This comprises:

> Proportional coverage and direction of article related to terrorism (Category A) from July to December, 2009 published in Time and Newsweek.

> Proportional coverage and direction of article related to Politics and Economy (Category B) from July to December, 2009 published in Time and Newsweek.

> Proportional coverage and direction of article related to Pakistan Military Operations (Category C) from July to December, 2009 published in Time and Newsweek.

> Proportional coverage and direction of Miscellaneous (Category D) from July to December, 2009 published in Time and Newsweek.

Part Two

This part is combination of both findings, qualitative and quantitative. This part has analyzed the data with discussion of both qualitative and Quantitative findings. It also provides the answer of research question on the findings of analysis and discussion.

5.1 Results of Articles Related to Terrorism (Category A)

Total number of article related to Pakistan during July, 2009 to December, 2009 published in Time and Newsweek are 128. In this time period numbers of articles related to terrorism (Category A) are 56 (43.75%). Whereas 29 articles are published in Time and 27 articles in Newsweek. This show that number of article related to terrorism published in Time is higher than Newsweek. Among 56 (43.75%) article related to terrorism published in July 5 (9%), August 6 (11%), September, 9 (16%), October 13 (23%), November 6 (11%) and December 17 (30%) published in both magazines. It shows that highest number 17 (30%) article related to terrorism published in December.

The direction of the articles related to terrorism (Category A) published in both magazines is in July 5 (9%) published whereas 1 article is positive, 3 articles are negative and 1article demonstrated the neutral direction, In August 6 (11%) articles published in both magazines in category A whereas 1 positive, 3 negative and 2 neutral, in September out of 9 (16%) have equal ratio of positive negative and neutral, in the month of October 13 (23%) positive 1, negative 9 and 3 are neutral, November shows that out of 6 (11%), 1 positive, 3 negative and 2 are neutral, December presents 17 (30%), 4 positive, 9 negative and 4 neutral.

Out of 56 articles related to terrorism published in both magazines from July to December, 2009; direction of 11(19.64%) articles are positive, 30 (53.57%) articles are negative and 15 (26.78%) are neutral.

Table 1: Articles Related to Terrorism (Category A) Published from July to December, 2009 in Time and Newsweek

Month	Magazines	No. of Articles Related to Pakistan	No. of Articles Related to Terrorism (Category A)	Direction of Articles (Category A)		
				Positive (+)	Negative (-)	Neutral (0)
July	Time	8	3 37.5%	1 12.5%	2 25%	0 0%
	Newsweek	8	2 25%	0 0%	1 12.5%	1 12.5%

August	Time	9	4 44.44 %	1 11.11%	2 22.2 2%	1 11.11%
	News week	10	2 20%	0 0%	1 10%	1 10%
September	Time	8	3 37.5%	0 0%	2 25%	1 12.5 %
	News week	10	6 60%	3 30 %	1 10%	2 20%
October	Time	15	8 53.33 %	1 6.66 %	6 40%	1 6.66 %
	News week	17	5 29.41 %	0 0%	3 17.6 4%	2 11.7 6%
November	Time	9	5 55.55 %	1 11.11%	2 22.2 2%	2 22.2 2%
	News week	3	1 33.33 %	0 0%	1 33.3 3%	0 0%
December	Time	14	6 42.85 %	1 7.14 %	3 21.4 2%	2 14.2 8%
	News week	17	11 64.70 %	3 17.6 4%	6 35.2 9%	2 11.7 6%
Total Six Month	Time	63	29 46.03 %	5 17.2 9%	17 58.6 2%	7 24.1 3%
	News week	65	27 41.53 %	6 22.2 2%	13 48.1 4%	8 29.6 2%
Total	Both Magazines	128	56 43.75 %	11 19.6 4%	30 53.5 7%	15 11.7 1%

Fig.1: Comparative Coverage of Article Related to Terrorism Published in Both Magazines

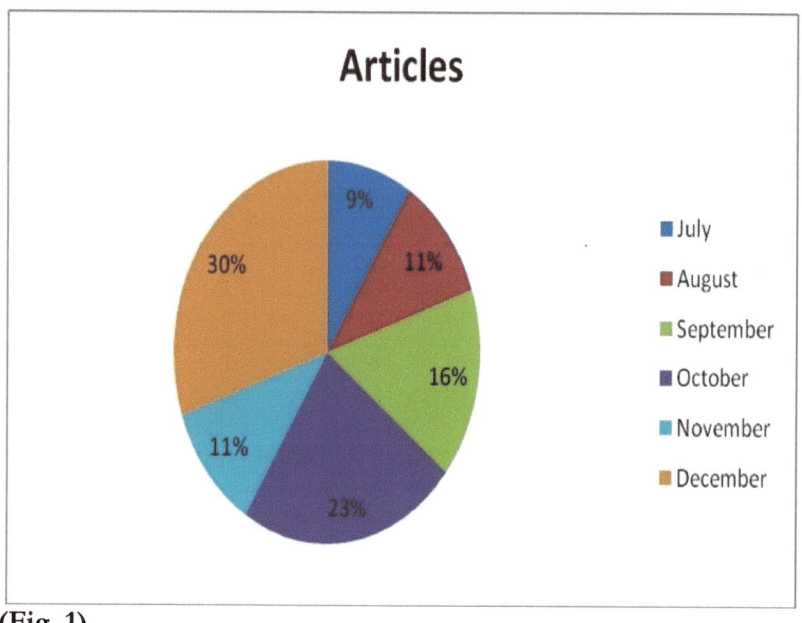

Articles

(Fig. 1)

Aggregate of article related to Pakistan during July, 2009 to December, 2009 published in Time and Newsweek are 128. In this time period numbers of articles related to Politics and Economy (Category B) are 28 (21.87%). where 11 articles in Time and 17 articles published in Newsweek. This show that number of article related to Politics and Economy published in Newsweek is higher than Time.

Within 28 (21.87%) article related to Politics and Economy (Category B), coverage of both magazines in July is 4 (14%), August 5 (18%), September, 6 (22%), October 6 (21%), November 1 (4%) and December 6 (21%).

The direction of the quality of articles related to Politics and Economy (Category B) published in both magazines is in July 4 (14%) published whereas 2 article are positive, 2 articles are negative and 0 article is neutral in direction, In August 5 (18%) articles published in both magazines in category B whereas positive 2, negative 1, and 2 are neutral, in September out of 6 (22%) positive 2, negative 1, and 3 are neutral, in the month of October 6 (21%) positive 1, negative 3 and 2 are neutral, November shows that out of 1 (4%), only 1 is neutral, December presents 6 (21%), positive 1, negative 3 and 2 are neutral.

Among 28 (21.87%) articles related to Politics and Economy (Category

B) published in both magazines from July to December, 2009; direction of 8(28.57%) articles are positive, 10 (35.71%) articles are negative and 10 (35.71%) are neutral.

Table 2: Articles Related to Politics and Economy (Category B) Published from July, 2009 to December, 2009

Month	Magazines	No. of Articles Related to Pakistan	No. of Articles Related to Politics and Economy (Category B)	Direction of Articles (Category B)		
				Positive (+)	Negative (-)	Neutral (0)
Jul.	Time	8	2 25%	1 12.5%	1 12.5%	0 0%
	New sweek	8	2 25%	1 12.5%	1 12.5%	0 0%
Aug.	Time	9	1 11.11%	0 0%	1 11.11%	0 0%
	New sweek	10	4 40%	2 20%	0 0%	2 20%
Sep.	Time	8	2 25%	1 12.5%	1 12.5%	0 0%
	New sweek	10	4 40%	1 10%	0 0%	3 30%
Oct.	Time	15	1 6.66%	0 0%	1 6.66%	0 0%
	New sweek	17	5 29.41%	1 5.88%	2 11.76%	2 11.76%
Nov.	Time	9	1 11.11	0 0%	0 0%	1 11.

						11%
	New sweek	3	0 0%	0 0%	0 0%	0 0%
Dec.	Time	14	4 28.57%	1 7.14%	2 14.28%	1 7.14%
	New sweek	17	2 11.76%	0 0%	1 5.88%	1 5.88%
Total July to December, 2009	Total Time	63	11 17.46%	3 27.27%	6 54.54%	2 18.18%
	Total Newsweek	65	17 26.15%	5 29.41%	4	8 47.05%
Total	Both Magazines	128	28 21.87%	8 28.57%	10 35.71%	10 35.71%

Fig. 2: Comparative Coverage of Article Related to Politics and Economy (Category B) Published in Both Magazines

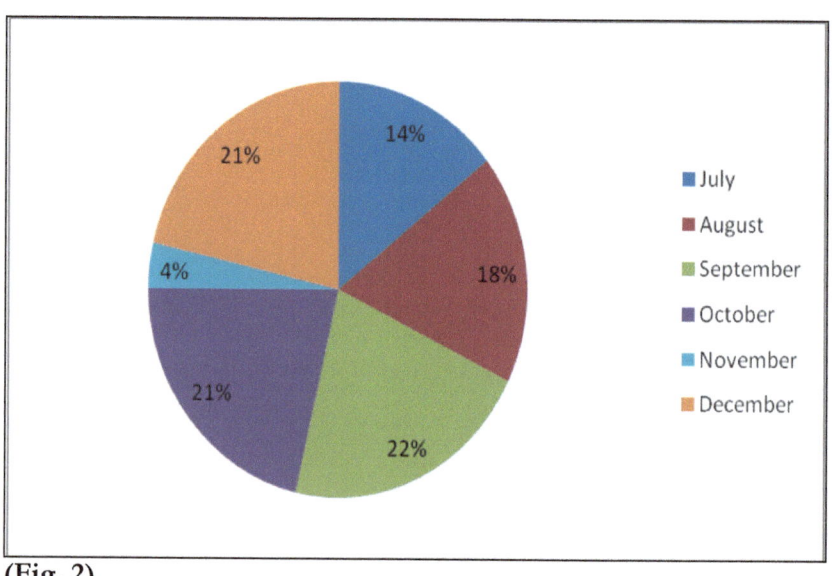

(Fig. 2)

5.3   **Results of Article Related to Pakistan's Military Operations (Category C)**

Total number of article related to Pakistan during July, 2009 to December, 2009 published in Time and Newsweek are 128. In this time period numbers of articles related to Pakistan's Military Operations (Category C) are 24 (18.75%). Whereas 14 articles in Time and 10 articles are published in Newsweek. This show that number of article related to Pakistan's Military Operations published in Time is higher than Newsweek. Among 24 (18.75%) article related to Pakistan's Military Operations (Category C) published in July 3 (12%), August 5 (21%), September, 3 (12%), October 6 (25%), November 4 (17%) and December 3 (13%) published in both magazines. It shows that highest number 6 (25%) article related to terrorism published in October.

The direction of the articles related to Pakistan's Military Operations (Category C) published in both magazines is in July 3 (12%) published whereas positive article 0, 2 articles are negative and 1 present the neutral direction, In August 5 (21%) articles published in both magazines in category C whereas 1 positive, 3 negative and 1 neutral, in September out of 3 (12%) positive 2, negative 1, and neutral 0, in the month of October 6 (25%) positive 2, negative 4 and 0 are neutral, November shows that out of 4(17%), 2 positive, 2 negative and 0 are neutral, December presents 3 (13%), 2 positive, 1 negative and 0 neutral.

Out of 24 articles related to Pakistan's Military Operations published in both magazines from July to December, 2009; direction of 9(37.5%) articles are positive, 13 (54.16%) articles are negative and 2 (8.33%) are neutral.

Table 3: Articles Related to Pakistan's Military Operations (Category C) Published from July, 2009 to December, 2009

Month	Magazines	No. of Articles Related to Pakistan	No. of Articles Related to P.M.O. (Category C)	Direction of Articles (Category C)		
				Positive (+)	Negative (-)	Neutral (0)
Jul.	Time	8	1 12.5%	0 0%	1 12.5%	0 0%
	News week	8	2	0 0%	1 12.	1 12.

					5%	5%
Aug.	Time	9	3 33.33%	0 0%	2 22.22%	1 11.11%
	News week	10	2 20%	1 10%	1 10%	0 0%
Sep.	Time	8	3 37.5%	2 25%	1 12.5%	0 0%
	News week	10	0 0%	0 0%	0 0%	0 0%
Oct.	Time	15	2 13.33%	1 6.66%	1 6.66%	0 0%
	News week	17	4 23.52%	1 5.88%	3 17.64%	0 0%
Nov.	Time	9	3 33.33%	2 22.22%	1 11.11%	0 0%
	News week	3	1 33.33%	0 0%	1 33.33%	0 0%
Dec.	Time	14	2 14.28%	1 7.14%	1 7.14%	0 0%
	News week	17	1 5.88%	1 5.88%	0 0%	0 0%
Total July to December,	Time	63	14 22.22%	6 42.85%	7 50%	1 7.14%
er,	News week	65	10 15.38%	3 30%	6 60%	1 10%
2009	Both Magazines	128	24 18.75%	9 37.5%	13 54.16%	2 8.33%

Fig. 3: Comparative Coverage of Article Related to Pakistan's Military Operations (Category C) Published in Both Magazines

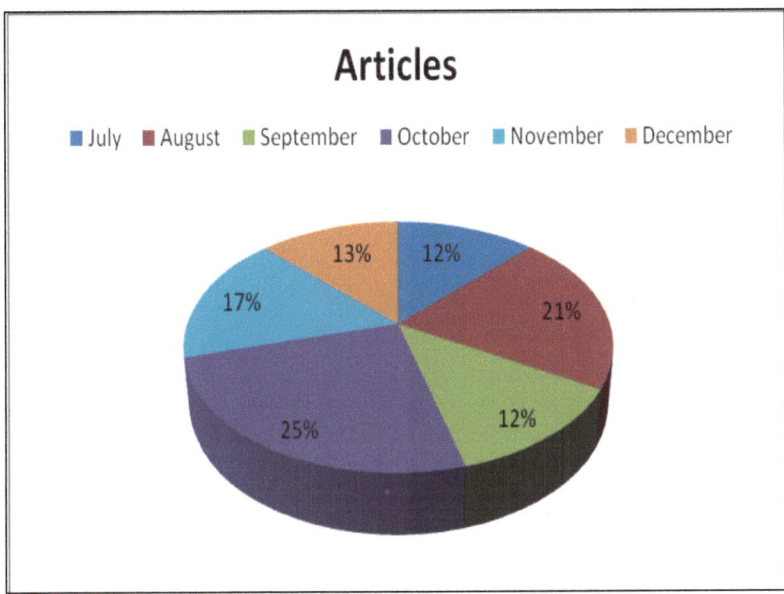

Articles

■ July ■ August ■ September ■ October ■ November ■ December

(Fig. 3)

5.4   Results of Miscellaneous (Category D)

Sum of article related to Pakistan for the period of July, 2009 to December, 2009 published in Time and Newsweek are 128. During this time period numbers of Miscellaneous (Category D) articles are 20 (15.62%). Whereas 9 articles in Time and 11 articles in Newsweek are published. This show that number of Miscellaneous article published in Newsweek is higher than Time. Among 20 (15.62) Miscellaneous article (Category D) published in July 4 (20%), August 3 (15%), September, 0 (0%), October 7 (35%), November 1 (5%) and December 5 (25%) published in both magazines.

The quality of direction of the Miscellaneous articles (Category D) published in both magazines is in July 4 (20%) published whereas positive article 2, negative 1, and 1 present the neutral direction, In August 3 (15%) articles published in both magazines in category D. Whereas, positive 1, negative 1 and 1 article is neutral, in September out of 0 (0%) having 0 article, in the month of October 7 (35%) positive 2, negative 5, and 0 are neutral, November shows that out of 1(5%), positive 1, negative and neutral are 0, December presents 5 (13%) are positive 2, negative 3, and 0 neutral.

Out of 20 Miscellaneous articles published in both magazines from July to December, 2009; direction of 8(40%) articles are positive, 10 (50%)

41

articles are negative and 2 (20%) are neutral.

Table 4: Miscellaneous (Category D) Published from July, 2009 to December, 2009

Mont h	Mag azines	No. of Articles Relate d to Pakista n	No. of Miscellane ous Articles (Category D)	Direction of Articles (Category D)		
				Po sitive (+)	Ne gative (-)	N eutral (0)
Jul.	Time	8	2 25%	1 12.5%	1 12.5 %	0 0%
	New sweek	8	2 25%	1 12.5%	0 0%	1 12.5%
Aug.	Time	9	1 11.11%	0 0%	1 11.11%	0 0%
	New sweek	10	2 20%	1 10%	0 0%	1 10%
Sep.	Time	8	0 0%	0 0%	0 0%	0 0%
	New sweek	10	0 0%	0 0%	0 0%	0 0%
Oct.	Time	15	4 2.66%	1 6.66%	3 20%	0 0%
	New sweek	17	3 17.64%	1 5.88%	2 11.76%	0 0%
Nov.	Time	9	0 0%	0 0%	0 0%	0 0%
	New sweek	3	1 33.33%	1 33.33%	0 0%	0 0%
Dec.	Time	14	2	0	2	0

			14.28%	0%	14.28%	0%
	New sweek	17	3 17.64%	2 11.76%	1 5.88%	0 0%
Total July to Dec., 2009	Time	63	9 14.28%	2 22.22%	7 77.7%	0
	New sweek	65	11 16.92%	6 54.54%	3 27.2 7	2 18.18%
		128	20 15.62%	8 40%	10 50%	2 10%

Fig. 4: Comparative Coverage of Miscellaneous (Category D) Published in Both Magazines

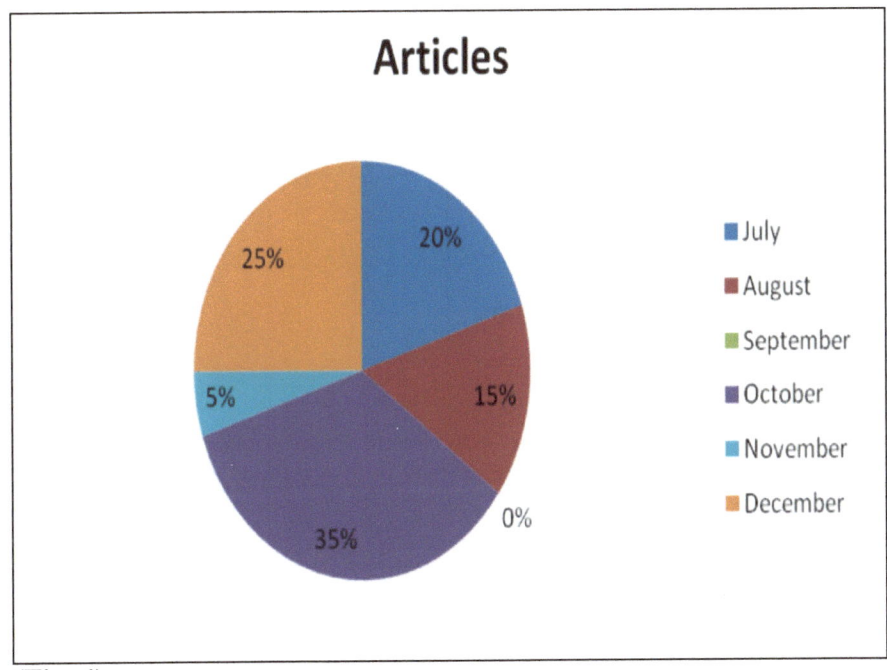

(Fig. 4)

5.5   Results of Comparative Direction of Categories of Both

Magazines

Cooperatively articles related to Pakistan published in both magazines are calculated here for final conclusion. Total numbers of Pakistan related articles are 128 where 56 (43.75%) articles are published in Category A, in Category B 28 (21.87%), category C 24 (18.75%) and Category D 20 (15.62%) articles. These four Categories express the direction and coverage of magazines that is, Positive 36 (28.12%), Negative 63 (49.21%) and Neutral 29 (22.65%).

Table 5: Comparative Direction of Categories of Both Magazines

Categories	No. Articles Related to Pakistan	Articles on Categorie's bases	Direction of Articles		
			Positive (+)	Negative (-)	Neutral (0)
A	128	56 (43.75)	11 (19.64%)	30 (53.57%)	15 (26.78)
B	128	28 (21.87%)	8 (28.75%)	10 (35.71%)	10 (35.71%)
C	128	24 (18.75%)	9 (37.5)	13 (54.16%)	2 (8.33%)
D	128	20 (15.62%)	8 (40%)	10 (50%)	2 (10%)
Total		128	36 (28.12%)	63 (49.21%)	29 (22.65%)

Fig. 5: Comparative Direction of Categories of the Both

Magazines

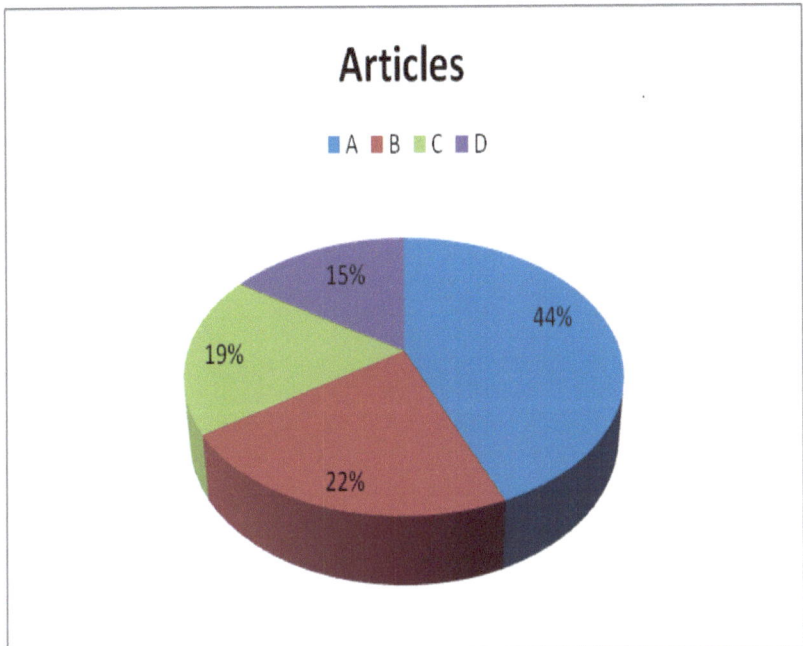

(Fig. 5)
Fig. 5.1: Comparative Quality of Categories of the Both Magazines

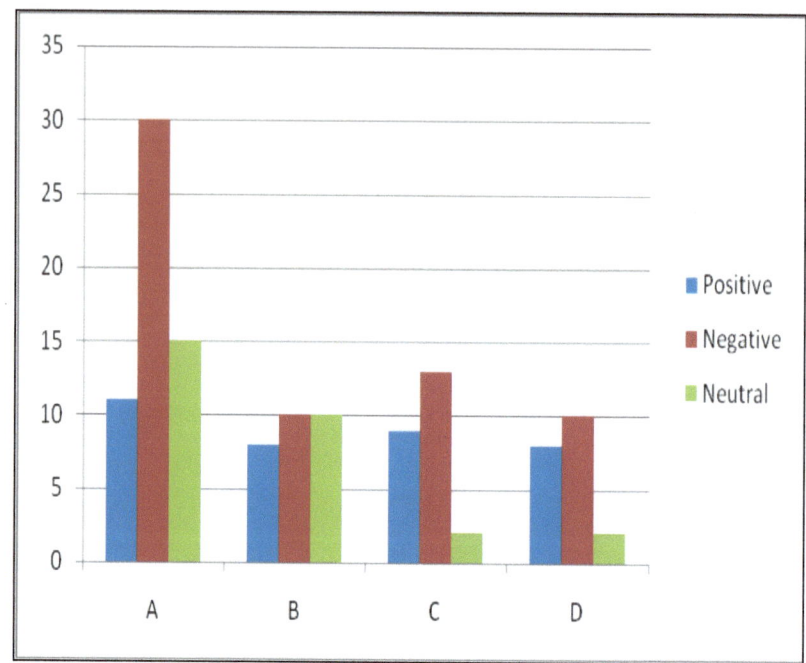

Fig. 5.1

.

6 RESULTS, DISCUSSION, CONCLUSION, AND RECOMMENDATIONS

6.1 Discussion and Results

US media has particularly portrayed the developing country image in his contents negatively giving a little attention. US media often used official biased source of information in the coverage of developing countries issues. The overall results of coverage of both magazines are not different. Pakistan is mostly covered negative than positive and more often frames are unfavorable than favorable. Pakistan was covered as an extremist country than a moderate state. Both magazines cover Pakistan as a political unrest country and base of religious terrorism. US media has often followed the state policy towards the developing countries. As Poorananda (1998) explains that US media depict Third World countries image negatively and mostly prefer to covers the issues related to disasters, failure of governments, conflicts and crime than art and science. There are several studies that show that elite American press coverage about foreign countries is biased by US policies (Zheang, et. all. 2006). Pakistan and US historical overview present that relations between two countries are at dagger drawn from the last three decades. Prior to the incident of 9/11 US policy toward Pakistan was critical. Khan (2008) finds out that,

"In the 1990s, the country had disposed of its democratically elected government in a military takeover, had set off nuclear weapons, and had engaged in war with neighbouring India. The US government had imposed sanctions and issued numerous critical statements about actions taken by Pakistani authorities. The editorial coverage of Pakistan in the late 1990s was decidedly on the negative side, just as earlier studies would suggest".

After 9/11 American policies toward Pakistan change the scenario, sanctions were lifted and statements about Pakistan's government relaying positively. But after the passage of time when Americans and NATO forces faced critical situation in Afghanistan and fail to counter with Taliban they start to blame on Pakistan that it is supporting to Taliban.

R. Q. What image the US leading news magazines portray?

Basically results of study support the assumption that portrayals of US leading news magazines portray Pakistan as negatively. No. of articles related to terrorism Fig. 1 showed that among the 56 (43.75%) articles related to terrorism 30 (53.57%) articles portray the negative image of Pakistan. Calculations of both magazines in category A, illustrate that majority of article are portrayed negatively. In category B article related to politics and economy of Pakistan portrayed as out of 28 articles 10 (35.71%) articles are negative and 8 (28.57%) are positive while 10 (35.71%) are neutral. This is because to that US media discuss that America is supporting to the falling economy and democracy in the country. Where US strategic concerns were related it depict that Pakistan has soft corner for Taliban. Mearsheimer (2009) in Newsweek wrote,

"Even if the U.S. military does pacify Afghanistan, moreover, Al Qaeda will still have its sanctuary next door in Pakistan. And Washington will face the same problem it did before 9/11; after all, those attacks could just as easily have been planned from Pakistan"

It also be depicted that Taliban are growing strong in the Pakistan and they could be able to hold the nuclear assets of Pakistan. Bailey (2009) wrote that, "administration's efforts more toward Pakistan reasoning that Al Qaeda—the real threat to the United States—is hiding out not in Afghanistan but in nuclear-armed –Pakistan".

In the category C article related to Pakistan military operations in Table: 3 presents that both magazines portray Pakistan as negative. In this category articles related to military operations of Pakistan 13 (54.16%) articles have negative direction, 9 (37.5%) have positive and 2 (8.33%) have neutral direction from the 24 articles. It present that the coverage about Pakistan military operations is covered negatively. As the CIA and US official's reports describes critically Pakistan role in war against terror. US magazines also portrayed these issues in favor of the State policies. As Time (2009) reported that,

"Pakistan is not betting on a U.S. victory in Afghanistan, nor is it going out of its way to help achieve one. Instead, say analysts and former top officials in Islamabad, Pakistan views the conflict in Afghanistan through the lens of its own national interests and its conflict with India — and it will act accordingly, prioritizing securing its own interests in Afghanistan's future. And that could be bad news for a U.S.-led military campaign that depends on Pakistan's help for thwarting the Afghan insurgency".

Category D that is based on general articles like religious, culture and art also resulted that majority of articles are portrayed the image of Pakistan negatively on the total 20 articles of this category only 8 (40%) article are positive and the 10 (50%) articles are negatively depicted. Over all findings of study prove the hypothesis as,

H: Most of the coverage given by the US magazines after 9/11 portrays the negative image of Pakistan.

Comparatively coverage of both magazines in the time period of July to December, 2009 showed in Table: 5 present that most of the coverage of Pakistan's image is negative. In the fig. 5.1 it is clearly showed that except category B all categories have the obvious ratio of negative image. Aggregate of the findings presented in Table 5 showed that there is significant ratio of negative image of Pakistan in 128 articles 36 (28.12%) were positive, 63 (49.21%) were negative and 29 (22.65%) were neutral.

6.2   Conclusion

This study tried to investigate the image of Pakistan in the US leading news magazines i.e. Time and Newsweek. These magazines have the wide circulation and vast readership in all around the world. Method of content analysis is used in finding the overall image of Pakistan in both magazines. Historically Pak-US relations saw many ups and down. Before the incident of 9/11 Pak-US relations was dagger drawn. As the horrific incident of 9/11 occurred Pakistan again gained attention of America and the whole world on war against Talban.

US government invaded on Afghanistan, an Al-Qaeda supported government to eliminate terrorism from the world. US charged that Osama Bin Laden al-Qaeda leader concealed himself in Afghanistan. Pakistan decides to join US war against terrorism in critical circumstances. Pakistan government provides all the possible support to America's and NATO forces. Pakistan army has launched military operations on its homeland against suspected terrorist on US demand. Pakistan successfully achieved the goal to eradicate the terrorist in its tribal areas. As NATO forces failed to control on insurgency and bomb blasts in Afghanistan. Change of US administration Bark Obama holds the presidency in 2009, his administration demand to Pakistan 'to do more' in war on terror. Besides the sacrifices of Pakistan military and public US departments and media start propaganda against Pakistan, as it is supporting Talban and has soft corner for religious extremist. Results of this study show that over all findings of both magazines portray image of Pakistan negative manner.

6.3   Recommendations

Through keen observation of this study researcher is able to suggest the following recommendations.

- ➤ US media persons should realize the facts and objectivity before the coverage of any issue related to terrorism and Pakistan.
- ➤ US leading news magazines i.e. Time and Newsweek should review their policies towards Pakistan, as Pakistan is a cordial ally of US on war against terrorism.
- ➤ Pakistan is already facing strike of terrorism, US media blame that Pakistan is friendly to terrorist its means that Pakistan willingly attempting suicide attacks on its forces and public.
- ➤ Impartiality and credibility should be attained by journalists in any circumstance in reporting the Pakistan's image.
- ➤ Policymakers of both countries should feel serious notice after this research about the relations of the both countries as well as the masses.
- ➤ Both magazines should try to ensure the balanced coverage in their content and persuade the issues positively.
- ➤ The researcher strongly recommends to the student of media sciences to explore the biased content of the western media.

6.4   Limitations of the Study

This study is limited to find out the image of Pakistan in the US leading news magazines. Time and Newsweek at the time period from July to December, 2009 were studied for this research. Study is conducted within limitation of time and sources. This study tried to focus on the articles related about the economic, political and military issues of Pakistan. It does not take into account the advertisements sections of the magazines for the purpose of study. Time and Newsweek these magazines selected due to vast readership. The 128 articles of both magazines from 1st July, 2009 to December 31, 2009 were analyzed for the purpose of study.

7 BIBLIOGRAPHY

1. Alger, D.E. (1989). The Media and Politics. New Jersey: Prentice Hall.p.126.

2. Ali, S. (2008). *US Mass Media and Images of Pakistan*. Vol. 10, http://www.acjournal.org/holdings/vol10/02_Summer/articles/ali.p hp. Retrieved on: January14, 2010.

3. Abbot, S. (2010). *Washington's refusal to talk about drone strikes in Pakistan.* http://pakistanherald.com/articles/Washingtons-refusal-to-talk-about-drone-strikes-in-pakistan-2196. Retrieved on: September 24, 2010.
    2/2/10)http://www.commondreams.org/headline/2010/02/02-7

4. Amir, A. (2001). *A Passion for Selling Ourselves Cheaply. Dawn*, 21 September 2001, http://66.201.122.226/weekly/ayaz/20010921.htm. Retrieved on: June 10, 2010.

5. Aukin, V. B. (2010). *Obama widens drone attacks in Pakistan. http://www.wsws..org/articles/2010/may2010/drone-m07.shtml.* Retrieved on: September 24, 2010.

6. Bailey, H. (2009). An Inconvenient Truth Teller http://www.newsweek.com/2009/10/09/an-inconvenient-truth-teller.html. Retrieved on: December 5, 2009.

7. Baloch, Q. B. (2007). *ENGAGEMENT AND ESTRANGEMENT IN US—PAK RELATIONS*, the Dialogue, Volume I, Number 4, 2007.

8. Baloch, Q. B. (2007). *ENGAGEMENT AND ESTRANGEMENT IN US—PAK   RELATIONS*, The Dialogue, Volume I, Number 4, 2007 p.41

9. Berelson, B. R. (1952). *Content analysis in communication research.* New York: The Free Press.

10. Berry, N.O. (1990), Foreign policy and the press: An analysis of The New York Times' coverage of US foreign policy, New York: Greenwood Press.

11. Bourdieu, P. (1998). *On television* New York: New Press.

12. Budd, R., Thorp, R. and L. Donohew. (1967). *Content Analysis of communication.* New York:Macmillian.

13. Bush, G.W. (1999). *Pakistan and Global War on Terrorism.* http://www.globalresearch.ca/index.php?context=va&aid=7746. Retrieved on: September 13, 2010.

14. Bush, G.W. (1999). Pakistan and Global War on Terrorism. http://www.globalresearch.ca/index.php?context=va&aid=7746. Retrieved on: September 13, 2010.

15. Charles T. Salmon, L.A. Post and Robin E. Christensen (2003). Mobilizing Public Will for Social Change; Michigan State University. Communications Consortium Media Center, Washingtion DC.

16. Chang, T. K. (1989). "The impact of presidential statements on press editorials regarding US-China Policy, 1950-1984", Communication Research, 16 (4), 486-509.

17. C.I.A., (2009). The world factbook.
     https://www.cia.gov/library/publications/the-world-
     factbook/geos/pk.html. Retrieved on: December 1, 2009.

18. Collins, L. (2008). UNITED STATES DIPLOMACY WITH
     PAKISTAN FOLLOWING 9/11. WWS 547: The Conduct of
     International Diplomacy. p.5.

19. Chong, D., Druckman, J. N. (2007). A Theory of Framing and
     Opinion Formation in Competitive Elite Environments. Journal of
     Communication 57 (2007)99–118, International Communication
     Association. P.102.

20. Cohen, C. (2007). A Perilous Cours, U.S. Strategy and Assistance to
     Pakistan: Center for Strategic and International Studies. 1800 K Street,
     N.W.Washington, D.C. 20006, Web: www.csis.org. Retrieved on:
     October 1, 2010.

21. Countrystudies. (2010). http://countrystudies.us/pakistan/81.htm.
     Retrieved on: August 9, 2010.

22. Dillard, J., Solomon, D., & Samp, J. (1996). Framing social reality:
     The relevance of relational judgments. Communication Research,
     23(6), 703-723.

23. Dunaway, J., Abrajano, M. A., Branton, R. P. (2007). Agenda
     Setting, Public Opinion, and the Issue of Immigration Reform.
     The Center for Comparative Immigration Studies CCIS
     University of California, San Diego: Working Paper 162 February
     2007

24. Edelman. M. (1993). Contestable categories and public opinion.
     Political Communication, 10,152-153.

25. Entman, R. M. (1991), "Framing U.S. Coverage of International News: Contrasts in Narratives of the KAL and Iran Air Incidents", *Journal of Communication*, 41(4), 6-27.

26. Entman, R.M. (2000). Declarations of independence: The growth of media power after the Cold War, in: Nacos, B.L. / Shapiro, R.Y. and P. Isernia (eds.): *Decisionmaking in a Glass House. Mass Media, Public Opinion, and American and European Foreign Policy in the 21ˢᵗ Century*, Lanham: Rowman&Littlefield, 11-26.

27. Fair, C. C. (2005). Demographics and Security: the contrasting cases of Pakistan and Bangladesh. Journal of South Asian and Middle Eastern studies. Vol.28, No 4, pp.53-76.

28. F.B.S., (2010). Federal Bureau of Statistics. Economy of Pakistan.

29. Folger,J. P., Hewes, D. E., and Poole, M. S. (1984). Coding social interaction. In B. dervin & M. J. Voigt. Progress in Communication Sciences, Volume IV, pp115-161. Norwood, NJ: Ablex.

30. Frey, L. R., Botan, C. h. and G. L. Kreps (2000). Investigating Communication: An Introduction Research Methods, second edition, printed in united state of America.

31. Gamson, W. (1989). News as framing: Comment on Garber. *American behavioral scientist, 33(2),* 157-161.

32. Gitlin, T. (1980). The whole world is watching: Mass media in the making and unmaking of the new left. Berkeley: University of California Press.

33. Glisi, J. (2009).The Role of Public Opinion and the Media in Civil Military Relations. http://www.google.com. Retrieved on: August 24, 2010.

34. Goffman, E. (1974). *Frame Analysis*, Philadelphia: University of Pennsylvania Press.

35.   Goffman, E. (1974). *Frame analysis: An essay on the organization of experience*. Cambridge: Harvard University press.

36.   Hackett, R. A. (1984). Decline of a paradigm? Bias and objectivity in news media studies. In M. Gurevitch & M. R. Levy. (Eds.). *Mass communication review yearbo*ok. (pp. 251-274). Beverly Hills: Sage Publication.

37.   Hashmi, R. S. (2007). WAR on Terrorism Impact on Pakistan's Economy. http://www.pu.edu.pk/polsc/jops/Currentissue-pdf/REHANA.pdf. Retrieved on: January 2, 2010.

38.   Holsti, O.R. (1969). Content Analysis for the Social Sciences and Humanities. Reading, MA: Addison-Wesley.

39.   Ipripak, (2010). Retrived August 26, 2010 from Ipripak :http://www.ipripak.org/factfiles/ff123.pdf.

40.   Iyengar, S., Peters, M.D., & Kinder, D.R. (1982). Experimental demonstrations of the "not-so-minimal" consequences of television news programs. The American Political Science Review, 76, 848-858.

41.   Jafri, T. (2009). Misleading statements can end Pakistan's credibility: http://www.globalpolitician.com/26026-pakistan. Retrieved on: July 6. 2010.

42.   Jameel, S. (2010). AMERICAN MEDIA POLICY FOR PAKISTAN. www.cgmentor.com/.../American%20media%20policy%20for%20Pa kistan.pdf. Retrieved on: September 13, 2010.

43.   Jasperson, A., Shah, D., Watts, M., Faber, R., & Fan, D. (1998). Framing and the public agenda: Media effects on the importance of the federal budget deficit. Political Communication, 15, 205-224.

44.   Kaplan, A. (1964). The conduct of inquiry. New York: Harper & Row.

45.   Kean, T. H., Hamilton, L. H., Ben-Veniste, R. (2005). Final Report on 9/11Commission Recommendations," 9/11 Public Discourse Project, December 5, 2005. http://www.9-11pdp.org/press/2005-12-05_report.pdf, 4. Retrieved on: March 12, 2010.

46.   Kempf, W. (2002). Conflict Coverage and Conflict Escalation. In Kempf, W. & Luostarinen, H. (Eds.), *Journalism and the new world order: Studying war and the media* (Vol. 2, p. 70). Goteborg University, Sweden: Nordicom.

47.   Kennedy, R. (1983). Testimony before two House subcommittees: http://www.fas.org/news/pakistan/1992/920731.htm. Retrieved on: August 1, 2010.

48.   Kerlinger, F. N. (1986). Foundation of Behavioral Research, (3rd ed.) New York, Holt, Rinehart and Winston.

49.   Khan, A. A. (2010). http://www.sixhour.com/pak-us%20ties%20in%20historical%20perspective.htm. Retrieved on: August 2, 2010.

50.   Khan, M. (2009). Pakistan's role in Global War on Terrorism. http://www.defence.pk/forums/strategic-geopolitical-issues/29111. Retrieved on: October 5, 2010.

51.   Khan, M. A. (2008). The Image of Pakistan in Prestigious American Newespaper Editorials: A Tes of the Media Confirmity Theory. http://www.issi.org.pk/ss_Detail.php?dataId=485. Retrieved on: October 20, 2010.

52.   Khan, R. M. (2010). http://pakobserver.net/detailnews.asp?id=24025. Retrieved on: July31, 2010.

53.   Kfir, I. (2009). U.S. Policy toward Pakistan and Afghanistan under the Obama Administration; http://www.gloria-center.org/meria/2009/12/kfir.htmlr. Retrieved on: August 3, 2010.

54.   Kronstadt, K. A. (2005). Pakistan-U.S. Relations Updated January 28, 2005 K. Alan Kronstadt Foreign Affairs, Defense, and Trade Division.

55.   Kronstadt, K. A. (2006). Pakistan-U.S. Relations Congressional Research Service, February 10, 2006.

56.   Krippendorff, K. (1980). Content Analysis: An Introduction to Its Methodology. Newbury Park, CA: Sage.

57.   Largio, D. (2004), "Uncovering the rationales for the war on Iraq: The words of the Bush Administration, Congress, and the media from September 12, 2001 to October 11, 2002", a Thesis at University of Illinois, Urbana-Champaign, IL.

58.   Lippmann, W. (1922). *Public Opinion*. http://www.google.com.pk. Retrieved on: May 6, 2010.

59.   Macnamara, Dr. J. (2006). Media Content Analysis. Paper Uses, Benefits and Best Practice Methodology: http://www.carmaapac.com. Retrieved on: September 21, 2010.

60.   Mearsheimer, J. J. (2009). Afghanistan: No More the Good War. http://www.newsweek.com/2009/12/04/afghanistan-no-more-the-good-war.html. Retrived on: December 4, 2009.

61.   Meet the Press, (2008). Meet the Press, December 8, 2008, transcript at http://www.msnbc.msn.com/id/28097635. Retrieved on: April 18, 2010.

62.   McCombs & Shaw. (1972). http://www.questia.com/googlescholar.qst; jsessionid. Retrieved on: December 12, 2009.

63. McCombs & Shaw. (2002). News Influence on our pictures of the World, in Media Effects edited by Bryant, J. and Zillman, D. UK: Lawerence Erlbaum Publishers. p.5

64. McChesney, R. W. (2002). The news media and world war III. In. M. Bromley., H. Tumber, B. Z. theory practice & criticism. Journalism, 3(1). Pp.14-21. London;sage.

65. McQuail, D. (1994). Mass communication theory: An introduction, 3rd ed., Sage, London. p.214.

66. Miller, K. (2002). Communication theories: Perspectives, processes, and contexts. McGraw-Hill: Boston. p.262.

67. Morgan, A. (2010). Running head: Beyond agenda setting. The Media's Power to Prime Critical Summary Paper. Middle Tennessee State University. http://mtsu32.mtsu.edu:11287/6000/morgan_summary.htm. Retrieved on: October 20, 2010.

68. Mouton, (2001). http://www.google.com.pk/search. Retrieved on: January 14, 2010.

69. Musharaf, P. (2006). In The Line of Fire, New York, Simon & Schuster.pp.158.

70. Musharraf, P. (2001). Speech to the nation, September 19, 2001.

71. Mushraff, P. (2006). In the Line of Fire. London: Simon & Schuster UK Ltd. pp.199.

72. Mushraf, (2001). Document 12, President Pervaiz Mushraf's address to the nation, September 19, 2001, IPRI, Journal, vol 11, No. 1 (Winter 2002) pp. 145-146.

73. Myers, M. (2000). Qualitative research and the generalizability question; standing firm with proteus. The qualitative report, 4(3/4). http://www.nova.edu/ssss/OR/OR41/myers.html. Retrieved on: September 23, 2010.

74. Newspapers, (2001). Dawn, Sep 14, 2001 See also The News, and Nation, Sept 14, 2001.

75. Neuendorf, K. (2002). The content analysis Guidebook, Thousand Oaks, CA: Sage Publications (P.9).

76. Nolan, R. (2006). Pakistan: The Most Allied Ally in Asia. http://www.fpa.org/newsletter_info2583/newsletter_info_sub_list.ht m?section=Pakistan%3A%20The%20Most%20Allied%20Ally%20in %20Asia. Retrieved on: September 13, 2010.

77. Pakistan. (2006). http://www.statpak.gov.pk/depts/fbs/publications/pocket_book200 6/general/introduction.pdf pakistan 2. Retrieved on: December 1, 2009.

78. Pakreview. (2010). http://pakreview.50webs.com/index_files/PakistanChannelsalpha.ht m. Retrieved on: December 1, 2009.

79. Pakreview. (2010). http://pakreview.50webs.com/index_files/PakistanNewspapersAlpha .htm. Retrieved on: December 1, 2009.

80. Pakistan, E.S. (2010). Economic Survey of Pakistan 2009-10.Chapter No.s 10, p 145,146.

81. Pak-US Business Council Report. (2009). http:www.uspakistan.org/. Retrieved on: August 13, 2010.

82. P.I.D., (2010). http:// www.pid.gov.pk. Retrieved on: August 9, 2010.

83. Poornananda, D. S. (1998). Coverage of South Asia in two leading US newspaper. Media Asia, 23930, 161.

84. Potter, w. J., Levine-Donnerstein, D. (1999). Rethinking validity and relaiblity in content analysis. Journal of Applied Communication Research, 27:3, p.266.

85. Raiz, S. (2008). The Relationship between the Public and Print Media Agendas on National Issues in Pakistan. Allama Iqbal Open University, Islamabad. p.38.

86. Raiz, S. (2008). The Relationship between the Public and Print Media Agendas on National Issues in Pakistan. Allama Iqbal Open University, Islamabad. p. 27-28

87. Raddatz, M. (2009). Department of State, "Interview with Martha Raddatz of ABC," press release, February 17, 2009.

88. Ramaprasad, J. (1984). "Foreign policy and press coverage: A study of the New York Times's coverage of India from 1973 to 1980", a Ph. D. dissertation at Southern Illinois University, Carbondale, IL.

89. Saleem, N. (2005). U.S. Media Framing for Foreign Countries Image: Canadian Journal of Media Studies, vol. 2910, 130. http:www.cjms.fims.uwo.ca/issues/02/01/saleem.pdf. Retrieved on: December 13, 2009.

90. Saleem, N. (2007). *Canadian Journal of Media Studies*, Vol. 2(1) http://www.aiou.edu.pk/gmj/TREATMENT%20OF%20IRAN -US%20STAND7.asp. Retrived on: October 5, 2010.

91. Salmon, C.T. (2003). Mobilizing Public Will for Social Change; Michigan State University. Communications Consortium Media Center, Washington DC.

92. Severin, W.J. & Tankard, J.W. (1997). Communications Theories: Origins, Methods, and Uses in the Mass Media. New York: Longman Publishers.

93. Shoemaker, Pamela & Reese, Stephen D. (1996), Mediating the Message: Theories of Influences on Mass Media Content, New York: Longman Publishing Group.

94. Starosta, W. J. (1984). Qualitative Content Analysis: A Burkean Perspective, pp. 185—94 in William B.Gudykunst and Young Yun

Kim (eds.), Methods for Intercultural Communication. Beverly Hills, Calif.: Sage.

95. Support, I. M. (2009). International Media Support. Published in Denmark by IMS.

96. The 9/11 Commission Report (2003).The 9/11 Commission Report, London, W.W.Norton Company. p.331.

97. Thyer, B. A. (1993). Single-systems Research Design in R.M/ grinnel (ed.),   Social Work. Research and Education. 94th ed. Illinois, F.E. Peacock Publishers.

98. Time, (2009). Why Pakistan Balks at the U.S. Afghanistan Offensive.
http://www.time.com/time/world/article/0,8599,1913151-2,00.html#ixzz0ugQCn8mT. Retrieved on: December 24, 2009.

99. Tiung, L. K., and Hasim, M. S. (2009). Media Framing of A Political Personality: A Case Study of a Malaysian Politician. European Journal of Social Sciences – Volume 9, Number 3. p.411. http://www.eurojournals.com/ejss_9_3_05.pdf . Retrieved on: September 26, 2010.

100. Tuchman, G. (1978). Xiang Zhou. "Cultural Dimensions and Framing the Internet in China: A Cross-Cultural Study of Newspapers' Coverage in Hong Kong, Singapore, the US and the UK", International Communication Gazette, 04/01/2008 .

101. Viking, (2007). Retrieved August 6,2010, from Viking: http://www.viking.ee/en/products/uksed/.

102. Vender, V. P. & Shoma, M. (2004).
http://www.isim.nl/noticeboard/fellow_detail.asp?n1=3&n2=4&n3 =0&fellow=324. Retrieved on: March 16, 2008.

103. Wikipedia, (2009). http://en.wikipedia.org/wiki/Newsweek. Retrieved on: January14, 2010.

104. Wikipedia, (2009). Retrieved August 6 ,2010, from Wikipedia: http://en.wikipedia.org/wiki/List_of_television_stations_in_Pakistan

105. http://www.fas.org/sgp/crs/row/RS22983.pdf (search by net)

106. Wikipedia, (2009). http://en.wikipedia.org/wiki/Time. Retrieved on: January 14, 2010.

107. Wikipedia, (2010). Drone attacks in Pakistan. http://www.wikipedia.org. Retrieved on: October 5, 2010.

ABOUT THE AUTHOR

Zafar Ali is PhD Scholar of Mass Communication at Gomal University D.I. Khan Pakistan. He completed his MS degree in Media & Communication Studies from International Islamic University Islamabad. Currently he is working as Community Awareness Officer at Punjab Emergency Service Rescue 1122 Pakistan. He is also author of number of research article published in world renewed research journals. Email zafaralizfr@yahoo.com

www.ingramcontent.com/pod-product-compliance
Lightning Source LLC
Chambersburg PA
CBHW050813290526
45792CB00001B/95